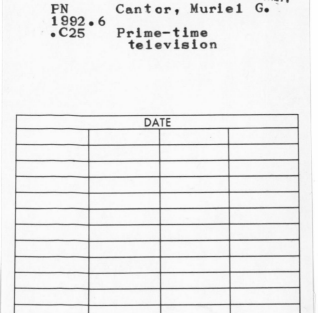

PN   Cantor, Muriel G.
1992.6
.C25   Prime-time
          television

DATE			

89011620

PRIME-TIME TELEVISION

The SAGE CommText Series

Editor:
F. GERALD KLINE
Director, School of Journalism and Mass Communication
University of Minnesota

Associate Editor:
SUSAN H. EVANS
Department of Communication, University of Michigan

This new series of communication textbooks is designed to provide a modular approach to teaching in this rapidly changing area. The explosion of concepts, methodologies, levels of analysis, and philosophical perspectives has put heavy demands on teaching undergraduates and graduates alike; it is our intent to choose the most solidly argued of these to make them available for students and teachers. The addition of new titles in the CommText series as well as the presentation of new and diverse authors will be a continuing effort on our part to reflect change in this scholarly area.

—F.G.K. and S.H.E.

Available in this series:

1. TELEVISION IN AMERICA
   George Comstock

2. COMMUNICATION HISTORY
   John D. Stevens and Hazel Dicken Garcia

3. PRIME-TIME TELEVISION: Content and Control
   Muriel G. Cantor

4. MOVIES AS MASS COMMUNICATION
   Garth Jowett and James M. Linton

additional titles in preparation

Muriel G. Cantor

PRIME–TIME TELEVISION
Content and Control

Volume 3. **The Sage CommText Series**

 SAGE PUBLICATIONS   Beverly Hills   London

To

Annette and Ephraim Baran

Copyright © 1980 by Sage Publications, Inc.

For information address:

SAGE Publications, Inc.
275 South Beverly Drive
Beverly Hills, California 90212

SAGE Publications Ltd
28 Banner Street
London EC1Y 8QE, England

Printed in the United States of America

Library of Congress Cataloging in Publication Data

Cantor, Muriel G
    Prime-time television.

    (Sage commtext ; v. 3)
    Bibliography: p.
    1. Television broadcasting--Social aspects--United
States. 2. Television broadcasting policy--United
States. 3. Television--Law and legislation--United
States. I. Title. II. Series.
PN1992.6.C25   302.2'3   80-12288
ISBN 0-8039-1316-8
ISBN 0-8039-1317-6 (pbk.)

FIRST PRINTING

CONTENTS

ACKNOWLEDGMENTS

This book is the result of ten years' work in the sociology of mass communications and the popular arts. The primary data from interviews with actors, Screen Actors' Guild and other union officials, directors, writers, and producers were collected in 1967-1968, 1970, 1973, and 1976. Many of the interviews with actors were conducted with Anne Peters, and Chapter 5 reflects our association. Another source of primary data is reported in Chapter 3. In 1972, I assisted the National Organization for Women in designing and carrying out a content analysis of one week of television as part of a petition to deny the license of WRC-TV. Because of that license challenge, I became interested in legal controls and the influences of citizen groups on the content of television programming.

The secondary data come from other studies on content and organizations associated with film and television, from congressional hearings and court decisions, and from newspaper and magazine articles about network officials, advertisers, and the creative personnel responsible for the episodic series and other television drama. These secondary data do not represent the entire universe of popular and scholarly material available on television drama. The literature on the subject is vast, and I have tried to select those court cases, articles, and other materials relating mainly to the control and selection of drama.

I am grateful to Paul Hirsch for suggesting that I write this book, to F. Gerald Kline for giving me the opportunity to do so, and to Susan Evans and Susan Soucek for editorial help and advice. Several of my students, Beverly Andrews and Leslie Smith in particular, provided me with insights on how the audience is conceptualized by various theorists. Others helped through the exchange of ideas. Joel Cantor, as usual, provided both editorial and substantive advice. The chapter on content could not have been written without using the unpublished materials provided by Lynda Glennon and Richard Butsch. Pauline Golden,

Catherine "Cat" Brady, and Kathleen Nolan of the Screen Actors' Guild, as well as the anonymous producers, writers, and actors must also be thanked. Most of all I am grateful to know and work with Anne Peters.

Reporters and social scientists have trouble presenting process. As I write, a new season of television drama is underway (1979-1980), and by the time this volume appears another season of drama will have been decided and made ready for distribution. I hope this book will provide insight into how such drama is produced and how societal and organizational forces have their impact on what people worldwide are provided for television viewing.

Muriel G. Cantor

Bethesda, Maryland

1

INTRODUCTION AND
OUTLINE OF INQUIRY

Focus of the book: how television drama, including situation comedies, action, adventure, and family series, are influenced by legal and political, organizational, and occupational milieus of production. Rationale and general outline of inquiry are provided.

Although everyone in the United States is familiar with television drama, few have examined the interlocking connection of its content with the social, political, and economic contexts of the creative process. Television drama is an ideal type of mass medium[1] to study because of the complexity of the production process[2] and the large audience it attracts, both in the United States (Sterling and Haight, 1978:377-378) and abroad (Tunstall, 1977; Schiller, 1969),[3] and because of the power attributed to its content by critics and scholars (Cater and Strickland, 1975; Report of the United States Commission on Civil Rights, 1977, 1979; Surgeon General's Scientific Advisory Committee on Television and Social Behavior, 1972; United States Congress, House, 1977).[4]

This book is the result of a ten-year study of the production of television drama, how it is produced, by whom, under what conditions, and for whom. In 1971, I noted that many researchers who have been most concerned with the effects of mass communications on American life, culture, and personality have repeatedly suggested that research focus on the communicator, the decision maker, and the structure of the entertainment industry (Cantor, 1971). After reporting on the work of on-the-line television producers, I conclude that how content is chosen, by whom, and under what social and political conditions remain complex questions that cannot be fully answered by studying one type of creator.

11

The dramas being examined are broadcast during the primetime hours (8:00-11:00 p.m.) by the three networks: The American Broadcasting Company (ABC), the Columbia Broadcasting System (CBS), and the National Broadcasting Company (NBC). These include the episodic series, movies made for television, miniseries, specials, and other serialized drama. All of these differing forms have several commonalities. They are usually produced in Hollywood (though occasionally elsewhere) by program suppliers who in name are independent of the television industry. As art, the critics consider these dramatic presentations low-level and standardized (see Gans, 1974:17-52). Their major overt function is to "entertain," not to educate or enlighten. They are made to attract large audiences in order to merchandise products. Of the various forms, the episodic series (including the situation comedies, action and adventure, and general drama) are considered the most profitable when successful. Each series episode or segment is usually a complete story; the main characters remain throughout a season or several seasons of broadcasting. When enough segments of a series are made, they can be rerun for additional profit, both in the United States and in other parts of the world.

Because of the importance of the series both as a form of culture and as a marketable product, most of the present analysis will be directed at their selection, creation, and dissemination. The prime-time series, movies made for television, and miniseries are not the only kinds of dramatic programs broadcast through commercial television. However, they are the only drama produced directly for television and shown in the evening. Not included in this analysis are other kinds of popular drama seen on television. These are movies made for theater distribution and later sold to the television networks and independent stations, the daytime serials (soap operas), and the animated children's shows (Cantor, 1972, 1974). The theater movies are financed, distributed, and created differently from drama made directly for television. The soap operas have much in common with the episodic series, but because they are usually shown on daytime hours rather than prime-time they are not as valued commercially. The soap operas continue a story from episode to episode, and therefore are more difficult to rerun or syndicate. As a form of popular culture, the soap opera is unique and deserves separate treatment. The genre accounts for large portions of the networks' income. However, an individual soap opera is never as profitable as a successful series (Cantor, 1979a).

Although there are indications that series may be less important as a cultural form compared with series of ten years ago, they are considered by many to be synonymous with American commercial television. Their profitability and their audiences may be declining because of the adoption of videotape home recorders, cable, and pay television. Also, the commercial value of series has decreased because more drama is produced locally in foreign countries. However, their influence from several perspectives cannot be denied; they are a model for foreign countries to emulate, contributing to the Americanization of culture worldwide (Tunstall, 1977:18; Schiller, 1969) and because of the claims concerning the effects of this drama on the behavior of the viewers, especially youths and children. Although series may be less important commercially than they were ten years ago, a successful series still commands a huge audience in the United States, and many series are still imported and shown abroad (Tunstall, 1977).

THE MODEL

The content and format of the series, the focus of this study, has been the object of widespread criticism from citizen groups and the press. More than ten congressional hearings have been conducted on the subject of television and violent content in drama since 1954 (Cater and Strickland, 1975; United States Congress, House, 1977). The content of television has been criticized by citizen groups for underrepresenting and stereotyping minorities and women and for showing too much explicit sex to a family audience (Report of the United States Commission on Civil Rights, 1977, 1979). For example, the Parent-Teacher Association devoted all of 1977 to the content of series, protesting the violence and sex and their effects on children and youths.

Much has been written on the content of series, but little on their selection, creation, and dissemination. There are, of course, articles on particular producers, writers, and actors: Newspapers regularly report the primetime and rating battles among the three major television networks. In the scholarly literature there are a few occupational studies of media creators of series but many content analyses (Franzwa, 1978). My study of producers (Cantor, 1971, 1972) and Faulkner's study of musicians (1971) are examples of the few studies of creators. There are problems when the focus is on an occupational group rather than on the selection process itself. Mass media communicators even in one society and in one industry are a heterogeneous group. The differences between the producers I studied and the musicians Faulkner studied are substantial when their power in the selection process and their orientation to work are considered. However, both studies show that the orientation of communicators is shaped not only by the tasks they perform and their attitudes and values, but by the *structures* and *culture* of the work organizations.

The Hollywood TV Producer (Cantor, 1971) focused on the work of the people creating prime-time series and how they are constrained by the organizational milieu and their work relationships. As mentioned above, this approach is limited. A research project in process explores the work of screen actors from a similar perspective (Peters and Cantor, 1978). These studies are similar to gatekeeper studies and studies of control of the work process. (As an example see Johnstone et al., 1976; also Hirsch, 1978a, for a review). In this study, rather than focusing on one occupation or organization, the total process will be examined.

The framework for this study is developed to show that the television drama is a product of exchange and struggle among several different organizations and groups (Cantor, 1979b). The model to be used is historical as well as systemic and interactive. Although the formula used by Harold Lasswell (1966), applied often in the past, has been useful for practical purposes, it has been rightly criticized because it is one-directional, not interactive and, therefore, restrictive. "Who says what to whom through what channels with what effects" ignores history; the industrial organizations responsible for the content; and the interaction between the audience, creators, and disseminators of the content (the "what" in Lasswell's model). Other systemic models such as those developed by John and Matilda Riley (1959) and Melvin DeFleur (1970) are more helpful because they are clearly interactive. Both the communicator and the audience are presented in a social context. However, both ignore history and have a common fault of system models; they ignore the strong influence of politics and economic power on creation and selection of content. In their favor, both, especially DeFleur, alert investigators to the complexities of content creation and selection. (See Lewis, 1978, for a review of the systems approach.)

The focus of the model will be the content. It is the content which has been extensively criticized by citizen groups, congressional committees, social psychologists, and other scholars and educators. Television is a relatively new medium. Although the technology was available before World War II, it was not until after the war that it became a national medium, replacing movies and radio, which have since become more specialized in their audiences (markets) and content. Although other kinds of television programs have also been the subject of criticism (especially commercial advertising and political messages), the content of television drama directed to both children and adults has generated the most intensive and extensive investigations and continuing concerns.

To set the stage, the study will begin with a review of how content has evolved and changed since the early 1950s. It will be shown that the form and content—the means of communications, actual story plots, and portrayals of people in series—have not remained static, but have and are changing over time. By combining the findings from content analyses with historical analyses of changing forms and messages, it is possible to discuss both change and continuity in series and other drama. It will be shown that anthologies, once popular, are no longer on the air; the evolution of the short series (miniseries) and the use of videotape instead of film still other examples of changing forms. The changes in messages are more complex and therefore will be discussed critically in some detail.

Most studies of content selection have shown how a program is conceptualized and carried through the various levels of production and dissemination (Gans, 1957; Elliot, 1972). Such studies are valuable because they provide examples of how the social context of production influences the final product. The gatekeeper studies mentioned earlier, while focusing on a single group (such as editors and censors), also show how the social norms, organizational structures, and culture influence the selection process (McQuail, 1969; Hirsch, 1978a). The model to be used in this study extends the meaning of the word "social" to include political and economic aspects of social life as well as the organizational, symbolic, and cultural.

Each succeeding section of the study will focus on parts of the larger interactive systems that contribute to the creation and selection of content. Within each section historical and contextual analyses will be combined. The model being used is borrowed in part from the one developed by Stewart and Cantor (1974) to look at the autonomy of workers. Autonomy is defined as the ability of workers to make independent decisions concerning the selection and creation of content.

If people working in the industry lack autonomy, they are limited in power and are subject to control from clients, organizations, other occupational groups, and the government at various levels. Social controls operate to modify or regulate the degree of autonomy experienced by individuals in their work activities and by organizations in their ability to carry out their perceived functions. Thus, social control is defined to include both formal and informal conditions limiting the actions of individuals, groups, and organizations. Formal controls may come from such societal arrangements found in the economic sphere and legal system. Informal controls come from the societal and cultural norms, values, and attitudes, such as those that have developed concerning sexual and violent content as a negative influence on viewers. Although it is impossible to account for all controls, it is possible to examine how autonomy is enhanced or controlled by the legal system, industrial organizations, creative people working in the industry, and the various publics and clients who view the series. Autonomy and power are being used interchangeably in this study. The question often asked is, "Who controls television?" (Seiden, 1974). The answer is those groups and creators who have the most power or discretion to make independent decisions concerning the content and dissemination of the programs.

The model is neither deterministic, nor does it emphasize stability rather than change. Although market conditions and the industrial milieu are seen as the major determinants of work behavior of the creators and thus the content, these conditions change as new technologies are adopted and as various markets (or publics) become more powerful. The controls at the societal level—the legal system—will be examined first; second, the organizational and economic controls that come from the networks; the sponsors and the local stations; and third, the occupational or creative controls. The final part of this analysis will examine the audience and the markets for television drama.

AN OVERVIEW—
LEVELS OF CONTROL

The Legal Context and Control

Most analyses of the media in America present a free enterprise system. The media are seen as existing at the pleasure of the government but autonomous from it. Such a perspective has several problems.

First, formal autonomy granted to the networks and production companies is taken at face value. It is rarely questioned how the networks, for instance, are free from regulation while the local broadcaster is not (see Head, 1976). Frequently, when the government is considered at all in communications research, it is seen as an outside influence which is trying to encroach upon the broadcasters' freedom to decide program content. A second problem with ignoring the role of the government as an influence on the selection of drama is that the interrelationship between media and government is an important feature in both developed industrial and developing nations. It is only more obvious and direct in some societies than in others. Therefore, for comparative and analytical purposes it is important to show (1) how the government has or has not supported broadcasters and production companies by the regulatory laws which have been adopted, (2) how court decisions have interpreted these laws, and (3) how critics and others have used Congress and the courts for redress of problems. A major contention in this study is that the first step in determining the content of popular drama is the law. The way the laws are written and interpreted are instrumental in providing the social milieu and support system for the final product. In the United States, because the legal system supports the marketing operations, the networks and production companies are more autonomous than the local broadcaster. Although it is recognized that the formal autonomy given by the government is not wholly responsible for the content, different controls and supports from the government would probably result in programming that is different from what is being shown on television today.

The Organizational Context

Regardless of who is in control of the means of communication— whether by the government directly, as in many of the socialist and third world countries, or those who own the various media, as in western democracies—the structure of the communication process is similar in one respect: Mass communications are organized (Wright, 1975). This means that the decision-making power to determine what is broadcast or printed rests with a very few people, and the creative people working in these settings do not necessarily express their own values, but rather the values of those in control of the bureaucratic structures (see Mills, 1953; Cantor, 1971; Johnstone et al., 1976). In the United States television drama is not produced directly by the stations broadcasting the programs. The production companies responsible for the series and movies made for television are located in Hollywood or New York. These production companies (program suppliers) are in name independent of the broadcast industry. This is a very important structural feature of the American broadcast industry. Another important feature is that the three commercial television networks are primarily responsible for financing and dissemination the drama. Finally, the networks are dependent on several large bureaucratically controlled organizations in order to produce shows that will be seen on the air. Rather than having a direct relationship with the viewing audience, the creators of television drama must satisfy at least one network, which in turn must convince the sponsors and local stations that the show will appeal to a large enough audience to make a profit or sell products.

In turn, television stations also are dependent on the networks, advertisers, and production companies. If a television station is affiliated with one of the three major networks, as are 85 percent of the commercial stations in the United States (Head, 1976), then a large segment of entertainment, news, and information programs are provided by the networks. If a commercial station is independent (not affiliated with a network), it must buy programs from syndication or distribution companies. Program suppliers occasionally sell original products directly to syndication companies. Norman Lear (TANDEM/TAT Productions) has done so in the last few years with some success and some failure. However, the program suppliers prefer selling to the networks because the profit is higher. Most of the shows broadcast on nonaffiliated commercial stations are reruns of programs which appeared on network television in the past. Syndication of already-run series and movies is very profitable; it is the ambition of every producer to have a series that is successful enough to be syndicated abroad as well as in the United States.

Creative Context and Control

The people who create series work directly for the program supplier or may themselves own the production companies. In Hollywood, where most of the series are made, there are a number of program suppliers, but three or four have become most powerful in recent years and control most of the production. Regardless of the size of the studio and the number of series being produced in one company, the actual production process varies little. The companies are dependent on the networks for financing, and all content is censored by the networks which broadcast the series. There have been changes in the ten years since I wrote *The Hollywood TV Producer* (Cantor, 1971) because of several antitrust actions and technological advances, but essentially the process of creation and selection remains the same. The networks decide what will be produced and how many episodes will be purchased; the production companies produce the series, using an on-the-line producer as the liaison between the network and production company and the creative people responsible for the actual filmmaking. From story to final print, many individuals play important technical and creative roles in filmmaking and contribute to the success of the films (and tapes). The on-the-line producer has authority over the selection of stories or series segments and the creative process. Actors, writers, and directors are directly responsible for the actual creative tasks and must satisfy the on-the-line producer, the program supplier (production companies), the networks, and, of course, finally some segment of the audience.

On-the-line producers, actors, writers, and directors claim they would like to make drama which is more artistic or more socially significant. Some think the networks underestimate the intelligence and taste of the audience; others think the existing audience is the only one possible for a medium that has as its essential function the merchandising of soap and patent medicine (Cantor, 1971, 1974). However, most see themselves as different from the audience and agree that they subordinate their own personal values and tastes in order to work. The parts people play and the stories written, directed, and produced are rarely chosen by the creative people responsible for their production. Only the unusual director or producer, writer or actor, one with considerable power in the marketplace, has the freedom of choice in the selection of content. Of course, writers who work on a freelance basis can write anything they wish. However, writing on specualation is a risk because it is difficult to find a buyer for a completed product. Most writers work on consignment, developing stories whose plots have been approved by the on-the-line producer and the program supplier, who act as filters for the networks which broadcast the programs. Because of increased showings of movies made for theater distribution and movies made for television, miniseries, and specials, there are fewer long series made each season. This means less work for the creative people. Thus, there is little opportunity to work in television dramatic production, and, when work is available, the creative freedom (autonomy) so greatly valued by the creators of cultural symbols is limited by the networks which select what will be produced, which censor content once a show is in production, and which have power over scheduling the show on the air.

Audience Control

The role of the audience in the determination of content is the subject of an ongoing debate. Some believe the influence of the audience is obscure and indirect (Gans, 1957; Riley and Riley, 1959). Others see the audience as having the primary responsibility for the content. Contributing to the lack of clarity in this debate is the difficulty in defining the audience. When the audience is seen as a mass, large and heterogeneous, it is difficult to make the direct connection between the audience and the content. The creation of a series takes place far in advance of the time it will be broadcast, and the only direct knowledge the creators have of the audience comes from ratings, letters, and commentary after the programs are shown. However, if viewers are conceptualized as markets and publics, the influence of the various groups can be put into social context. For example, citizen and pressure groups are trying, and have tried in the past, to gain access to television drama in order to present their particular point of view. These pressures on the creative people, the networks, and the local stations have increased in recent years. While both program suppliers and network officials claim their rights to self-regulation and freedom of speech, the intensified efforts of several powerful groups have had an impact on both the work of creators and the content they create (see *TV Guide*, 1977).

There are many examples of pressure group activities, but those concerned with television violence have been the most active in pressuring for change in television drama. The groups concerned with the portrayal of women and minorities have from 1970 on also been making a concentrated effort to bring these issues to the attention of the networks, Congress, and the Federal Communications Commission (Report of the United States Commission on Civil Rights, 1977, 1979). Based on studies conducted by social scientists, the rationale used by those concerned with the portrayal of women and minorities and those concerned with violence is similar. Concerned groups argue that a great deal is taught indirectly and by example about attitudes, values, and self-perception, and that television drama serves literally as a model of reality for countless children and youths. The more radical critics see the dramatic content as an instrument of political oppression because it systematically excludes, ridicules, regulates, and stereotypes members of minority groups and women (Leifer et al., 1974).

While critics lament the sex, violence, and stereotypic treatment of women and blacks, the market audience continues to watch programs in large numbers. Therefore, it is important to reconcile the criticism of various publics and citizen groups with the continuing popularity of the drama. Market decisions about what to select are based on a number of factors, but the primary factor in keeping a series on the air once it is selected is the ratings.

The argument being made is that both the form and actual content of prime-time programs depend on social and political controls which exist outside the creative process. At present, the networks have the greatest power over the creators, but critics and social action groups through continuing pressure have increased the government's involvement in television production. Also, several court decisions have increased the power of the government and the production companies. The adoption of new technologies—particularly the adoption of video-tape for home use, cable, pay-TV, and others—could also contribute to weaken the control exercised by the networks over drama. It is clear from the history of the broadcasting and film media that regulation and content are not static; rather, changes occur as industrial and market conditions change, and these are part of larger economic, political, and social processes.

OUTLINE OF THE BOOK

To set the stage for the elaboration of the model being used, Chapter 2 examines the content of television drama. Chapter 3 focuses on the legal context and controls; Chapter 4 on the economic and organizational contexts associated with the production of television; and Chapter 5 on the creative controls over work in filmmaking. Chapter 6 considers the relationship of the audience to the production of drama. This chapter is somewhat different from the others because various theoretical perspectives will be elaborated. The power of the audience over the creation and selection of drama is conceptualized differently by scholars and investigators, depending on the specific theoretical or political orientation of the investigator. The conclusion, Chapter 7, provides a summary and discusses the relationship of drama to technology and how the adoption of new technologies might influence the social organization of production.

Although this book has been developed as an integrated work, each chapter can be used individually for classroom purposes, depending on how an instructor organizes a course. Chapter 6, because of the review of mass society theories, radical perspectives, and social organizational approaches, is particularly useful as an introduction to the study of mass communications generally.

NOTES

1. See Wright (1975:4) for a definition of mass communications. I prefer the term mass media (or medium) of communications. As will be clarified throughout, generalizations about the media can be made, but it is more fruitful to study a medium for comparative purposes and for enlightenment about questions of power, control, and influence.

2. The major organizations contributing directly to the production of television drama are the three television networks—(ABC), (CBS), (NBC)—who control the means of communication, the sponsors and advertisers who provide the financial base for the programs, and the program suppliers (studios) who actually create and produce the shows. Indirectly contributing to the production of drama are the social critics and pressure groups, the rating services which measure the audience, the syndication companies and distributors, and the legal supports and constraints. (These are not listed in order of importance.)

3. Not all shows attract large audiences. However, the audience sizes for some dramatic productions have been enormous. For example, 120,000,000 people watched one or more episodes of *Holocaust* during the winter of 1978. *Roots* drew even a larger audience (Sterling and Haight, 1978).

4. I will report the criticisms, but will not evaluate whether they are correct. The critics are important because they show how much influence is attributed to this kind of drama (also see Cantor, 1979b).

2

FORM AND CONTENT

How the various forms of television drama evolved. What is
known about content and how it is studied and criticized.
Changes in form and actual message since 1954 when Hollywood became the major production center for television
drama.

This book is about primetime drama presented through commercial
television. The focus of the book will show how drama is created and
the power associated with the selection of this drama for viewers.
Before issues relating to dissemination and production are addressed, it
is necessary to explain what is meant by prime-time drama and why its
production and dissemination are important to study. Prime-time
drama includes those dramatic programs which have been produced
directly for television and which are broadcast originally during the
evening hours, usually between 8:00 p.m. and 11:00 p.m.[1] For this
study, drama is any entertainment television program involving a story,
plot, or character development which is considered fictional in nature.
Furthermore, to qualify as drama, the play must be a full-length
program, usually one-half hour or longer in length; skits presented in
variety entertainment programs do not qualify. Most drama presented
on television could be produced on the stage with little change. All can
be presented in theaters because they are on film or videotape. Drama
includes fictionalized accounts of actual events, comedies, tragedies, as
well as general drama.

Some justifications for examining drama separately from other television programs were given in the introductory chapter. Television
drama is probably the most widely accepted form of entertainment ever
conceived; it has been called the "most popular art" (Newcomb,

1974). Drama is viewed both nationally and internationally by hundreds of millions. Although this drama is very popular both in the United States and abroad (see Tunstall, 1977; Wells, 1972), it also widely criticized and rarely acclaimed. As a form of culture it is important because most (not all) analysts see television drama as containing negative symbols which dominate American society. It is claimed by many that these negative symbols have serious consequences for those who make up the audience. The perceived negative symbols and the consequences these may have for viewers will be discussed later in the chapter. To be more specific about the genre and to tie the content to the criticisms, this chapter will be divided into three parts. The first section explains the various types of drama and how they evolved. In the second section, there will be a review of what is explicitly known about the content; how it has been studied; and how critics justify their claims about the prevalence of violence, sex role, occupational, and minority stereotyping. The third section will contain a discussion about how drama has changed both in form and message.

DRAMATIC FORMS

Background

Commercial television is not only an industry producing culture, it is also an industry that generates profit. Although one of the major functions of commercial television is to provide information in the form of news, public affairs programs, and political materials, the most profitable kinds of programs are those which have been considered "mere entertainment" (see Leifer et al., 1974). As Elihu Katz (1977) has noted, most people originally bought television sets to be entertained. From the earliest days of commercial television in the United States, drama has been the primary method of entertaining viewers. The reasons for the popularity of drama have been widely recognized but rarely explored analytically. Compared with other kinds of entertainment programs such as variety shows, quiz and game shows, and sports events, drama continues to be the main source of profits for the three networks. Television drama has both cultural and commercial value that other kinds of entertainment shows do not have. When successful, television shows are profitable not only through original showings, but through syndication for additional showings and subsidary profits from phonograph record sales, posters, clothing, and other artifacts that can be licensed to manufacturers, using the star actors or the show itself as a selling device. The cultural value of the shows is not as easy to demonstrate. The range of themes, plots, and symbols that can be communicated through drama is obviously large. Drama can have many functions: It can be used as a vehicle for propaganda, for showing changing social relationships in society, and for presenting information in an engaging and entertaining way. It provides fantasy and escape from the mundane and ordinary as well as conflict and consensus.

Although it can be argued that television drama is transient in comparison with other art forms, it is the least transient programming type transmitted through television. Once videotaped or filmed, it can be and often is shown many times and in many different places. Television drama is both an art form and an economic commodity. When studying drama, it is difficult to separate its value as culture from its economic value; as both, it is significant. Because this drama is so highly valued by certain business interests and so widely criticized by intellectuals, the content of drama has generated many controversies and conflicts (Cantor 1979a).

History

Prime-time commercial television drama has three direct antecedents: one is commercial network radio drama of the 1930s and 1940s, the second is the American theater film (the movies), and the third is the American theater. Network radio dramatic forms have been the most influential, followed by the motion picture. The American theater has been the least influential but the most glorified. Commercial television broadcasting became a competitor for the movie industry and national network radio shortly after World War II (see Barnouw, 1970 and 1977, for a history of commercial television in the United States). The earliest dramatic programs were produced live in New York broadcasting studios. These early programs were either anthology series; a complete play shown each week; or what Eric Barnouw calls the episodic series, chapters of a larger story usually on the air weekly. The live anthologies were greatly acclaimed by critics; the episodic series were the focus of criticism from the time they appeared on the air (Cater and Strickland, 1975). From about 1945 to 1951 all drama was produced live in New York studios. Most of this drama has disappeared, although a few kinescopes (films of the live productions) remain. Starting in the early 1950s some drama was being filmed in Hollywood; by the end of the decade practically all dramatic shows were filmed in studios that formerly had been used to produce Hollywood movies. Although there are dramatic shows made on location (*Hawaii Five-O* for example) or in New York, most are still either filmed or videotaped in Los Angeles.[2] While the shows are primarily financed by the three major television networks, they are created by people associated with the film industry (see Chapters 4 and 5). As will be detailed, present-day television drama represents the marriage of network radio and the American film industry.

The Anthologies

In the early days of television broadcasting live anthology series on the air were theater plays adapted for television. At one time during the early 1950s there were 18 such live anthology dramas on the air (Barnouw 1977; Avery, 1977). Each of these was a dramatic series with an original play and different cast each week. The live anthology has practically disappeared from the air, and only rarely will a theater play or a special production be filmed or videotaped for transmission through television as a special event.[3] The anthologies were well received by the critics of television, and the era in which they appeared is now called the Golden Age of Television (Barnouw, 1970, 1977; Avery, 1977). The form was flexible, varied, and invited experimentation. The plays were shaped by the advertisers (sponsors) who in the beginning granted creative freedom to the writers and directors.[4] Diversity of plot rather than formula associated with series drama (Newcomb, 1974) was the key distinguishing feature of these anthologies. According to Barnouw (1977), the play was the thing and actors were chosen to fit the play, not vice versa, as is the case with most episodic series and more recent television drama.

Among the 18 anthologies on the air during the 1952-1953 season when the Federal Communications Commission lifted its ban on television licenses were *Philco Television Playhouse, Goodyear Television Playhouse, Kraft Television Theater* and *Armstrong Television Theater.*[5] As these names illustrate, most anthology series were named after the company sponsoring the series. The plays were so varied that few generalizations can be made about their content. Although this period is considered the Golden Age of Television, some aspects of the production have been criticized. Women were clearly given a smaller proportion of the roles than were male actors (see Head, 1954). It was unlikely that a black would appear in any role other than servant or entertainer (Report of the United States Commission on Civil Rights, 1977). Moreover, the sponsors directly responsible for the productions were intimidated by the anticommunist sentiments prevalent at the time. Writers, actors, and directors were targeted for attack by anticommunist groups. One anticommunist group became especially powerful. A publication called *Red Channels* (American Business Consultants, 1950) was published by *Counterattack*, self-described as a newsletter of facts to combat communism. *Red Channels* listed the names of 151 writers, directors, and actors considered among the most talented in the industry, claiming these people were communist sympathizers. Afraid of offending the buying public, the advertising agencies who sponsored the dramatic anthologies and other dramatic programs blacklisted many whose names appeared in *Red Channels* (American Business Consultants, 1950; Barnouw, 1977).

In spite of the control exercised by the advertisers, there is consensus that originality was highly valued during the early days of television. Several writers wrote teleplays that have become classics. *Marty* which appeared on *Goodyear Television Playhouse* in 1954 is one example; another is *The Miracle Worker*. *Marty* later became a major theater film and launched its writer, Paddy Chayefsky, on his career. He became one of the top script writers of teleplays and, later, films. *The Miracle Worker* went through an unprecedented metamorphosis from the original television drama to a Broadway play to a motion picture and returned to television as a special in the fall of 1979. Arthur Penn, the director of *Bonnie and Clyde*, directed the first production of *The Miracle Worker* for *Playhouse 90*.

The Golden Age of Television only lasted a few years. According to Barnouw (1977: 165), during the 1954-1955 season, sponsors no longer granted freedom to writers and directors but began to interfere with the scripts and plots. Those who had been attracted to the medium because of the creative freedom turned elsewhere to have their work produced, some to the movies and others back to the theater. The anthologies began a rapid decline. Sponsors were switching from live presentation to films produced in Hollywood. In 1955 *Philco Playhouse* moved to Hollywood and others followed. *The U.S. Steel Hour* survived the longest of the live anthologies. However, by the 1960s almost all drama was being filmed, and most anthology series, whether live or on film, no longer existed. The episodic series became the dominant form of drama seen on television.

The Episodic Series

The episodic series represents the marriage of the Hollywood movie industry (production) and network radio (format). An episodic series is a dramatic show, usually one-half hour or one hour long; most appear on the air on a weekly basis. The main characters continue from episode to episode, and each segment is usually a complete story revolving around the main characters. The star often becomes the most important person in the drama, and many series bear the name of their star or the fictional name of the character played by the actor. The series itself has a basic story concept that helps determine the content of each segment. This concept is usually relatively simple so that various complete stories can be told each week.

Successful series have a story concept broad enough to allow a number of adventures or incidents to be created as episodes and a star or stars who are attractive to the audience. Series have been failures, according to those I have studied, because the story line was not right for the series format. For example, a pilot film for one series revolved around a saleswoman who inherited a million dollars. Once the character's wealth was established, the writers found it difficult to produce plots that kept the original storyline intact. The series failed in its first season because the teleplays were simply about another rich woman who had little or nothing to do with her inheritance. The importance of the stars is discussed in Chapter 5.

Episodic series are different from the weekly movie serials that were shown during the Saturday matinees to children in the 1930s and 1940s (Stedman, 1977) and other serialized fiction such as daytime radio and television serials (soap operas). The cliff-hanger serial of the movies, the serialized novel which appears in magazines and newspapers, and the soap opera consist of stories which continue from segment to segment. Most prime-time series are complete chapters and can be rebroadcast in any order. A few serialized dramas that approximate the soap opera are shown in prime time, but the form is not as profitable for broadcasters in the evening hours as it is during the day (Cantor, 1979a). The format of the episodic series makes it resaleable for syndication. Many old series are presently on the air which have been broadcast before. All soap operas in the United States are usually seen only once—during their original daily broadcast (Cantor, 1979a). A major consideration in developing a series is whether the story will lend itself to the chapter format. Although *Peyton Place* (1964-1969), the most successful prime-time soap opera drama, consists of 514 episodes, it has not been sold for syndication in the United States. On a weekly basis there are enough episodes of *Peyton Place* to run for ten years, at 52 episodes a year (Stedman, 1977:412). At the present time, there are several serialized dramas on the air which qualify as soap operas: *Soap* and *Dallas* are examples. If such dramatic shows are syndicated in the future, the order in which the segments are broadcast will be important.

Both the episodic series and the soap opera had their origins in network national radio. The first nationally broadcast drama was *Amos 'n' Andy* which essentially can be considered a soap opera. The characters Amos and Andy were rustic blacks although they were originally played by two white men. *Amos 'n' Andy* had been on the radio in Chicago when in 1929 the NBC radio network began to broadcast the program six days a week for 15 minutes. The program was a phenomenal success, probably the most successful radio series ever presented. It went from a 15-minute radio series to a half-hour variety program to a television series. As a television series it was ill-fated because of charges of racism in the stories by the black men who played Amos and Andy (Stedman, 1977:229-232).

The episodic series format was also introduced to radio around 1929 by several different advertisers. Several weekly series were broadcast on both television and radio in the early 1950s. *Gunsmoke* (1952-1961 in network radio and 1955-1975 on television) is the longest-runing evening program. However, *Dragnet,* the *The Aldrich Family,* and others were first radio series and later or simultaneously became television series in the 1950s. Because these programs and the soap opera came directly from radio, television drama in its early days was considered radio with pictures. All radio drama, whether categorized as a series or a soap opera, had one thing in common: the drama was designed to consider the commercial break at the end of each 15-minute segment. Many radio dramas started as 15-minute programs and simply expanded by adding segments. This feature of radio has been carried over to and has influenced the form of television. No matter how long a program is on the air each week, most programs break every 15 minutes (actually less, after 12 minutes of program) to give time for the local station to identify itself and for both local and national commercial advertisements. The commercial advertisements essentially pay for the drama and accrue profits for the stations and networks. Because of the short time allowed for dramatic action, writers have learned to compress action. More important, the material is written so that the viewer will be drawn back to the show after the commercial break.

Episodic series have been the mainstay of commercial prime-time broadcasting since 1954. As a form they have many advantages for the commercial medium. Their most important advantage is that they may be rerun many times and in any order. Episodes which do not meet the approval of the local broadcaster can be dropped without breaking the continuity. Although the anthology form survived to some extent on film and through special productions, the episodic series is preferred by most sponsors. Identification with a continuing, attractive actor has several merchandizing advantages for the networks and the sponsors. Also, series are written to a formula which offers security for the sponsors and possibly the viewers as well. Each episode or segment is a variation of an approved ritual, and usually solutions to conflicts and problems are clear-cut. The sponsors and the audience know what to expect. Moreover, series can be used as a way to pretest new shows by introducing characters and plots that serve as pilot films. Popular secondary characters may be assigned a series of their own, a development known as a spin-off.

There are several kinds of episodic series, but it is difficult to categorize them because many can be considered mixed. Most reviewers distinguish four major categories: the western, the detective or mystery, situation comedies, and general drama (a catch-all category). Horace Newcomb (1974), who has described television drama in some detail, divides drama into four types: situation and domestic comedies, mysteries (shows about order and authority) doctors and lawyers, and adventure shows. Joseph R. Domminick and Millard C. Pearce (1976) note that finding categories that adequately describe television content is a problem that has continually vexed social scientists (as well as producers of Emmy Awards). Even the rating services, such as the A.C. Nielsen Company, have difficulty deciding programming categories. Although in this analysis the mixed nature of many dramas is recognized, it is important to distinguish the situation and domestic comedies from the action-adventure shows (westerns, mysteries, detective and others) and general drama. The reasons for distinguishing at least two types will be clarified throughout the chapter.

Hollywood and TV Drama

Although radio drama provided the format and form for television series, the Hollywood movie industry provided the product. In the beginning of television, the movie industry was aloof to overtures from the television networks who needed programs to fill airtime. Not only did most movie studios withhold old movies by not allowing them to be sold for televiewing, but they refused to enter into production agreements with either the networks or advertising agencies which had provided radio programming. However, because most studios were suffering financially, they were willing to rent space to independent producers who proliferated in the early 1950s in Hollywood. This began to change in 1954, when ABC made a deal with Walt Disney for a Disneyland series.[6] In the 1955-1956 season, Jack Warner undertook to produce films for ABC-TV. The most successful of these, *Cheyenne*, became a network staple for seven years. Because well-known actors shunned television, Clint Walker, previously an extra, was cast in the leading role and established himself as a star. *Cheyenne* was so successful that carbon copies became highly marketable. From the beginning each network followed the other when a particular type of program became popular.

The years 1955-1956 brought *Wyatt Earp, Gunsmoke, Tales of the Texas Rangers, Death Valley Days, Frontier, Broken Arrow, Adventures of Jim Bowie* and others to television. After Warner Brothers capitulated to network pressure, MGM, Twentieth-Century-Fox, Paramount, Columbia Pictures, and United Artists started to either produce television drama or sell old movies to television. These studios were the largest and most powerful in the heyday of Hollywood. Although they did not put the effort into television series that was being put into the movies, the profit from network sales and residuals were important in keeping the Hollywood film industry alive. Some studios did fail, and all cut down production. Eventually, Paramount was bought by Gulf-Western, Universal by MCA, and Warner Brothers by Kenney (who changed its name to Warner Communications). Large movie lots were sold off to commercial builders, and by 1970 most of the studios that remained in Hollywood rarely made theater films. Rather, most Hollywood studios produced (and are still producing) films and tapes for the television networks.

The television adventure series used the old large stationary cameras, were rarely filmed on location, and, because of the cost, used stock footage when expensive action scenes were called for. Most series, however, had small casts compared with the old action Hollywood movies and their "casts of thousands." A half-hour series is usually filmed in five days, which prohibits the perfection of scenes through retakes that contributed to the fine production quality associated with class A Hollywood films.

The comedy series developed differently from the action series. The story of *I Love Lucy* is the best example of influence of both radio and the movies on television. *I Love Lucy* was originally filmed in a studio rented by Lucille Ball and her husband Desi Arnaz in 1951. The technique used to film the show provided a new flexibility for the series being made for televiewing. From its inception, the show was filmed with three cameras in front of a live audience. This technique allowed the entire play to be presented in sequence for the live audience, and editors selected the best shot from the three films for the home viewing audience. Even after the video camera became the medium for the domestic and situation comedy, the method developed by Lucille Ball and Desi Arnaz was commonly used. Now most comedies are video-taped in studios in front of live audiences, but still use the multiple camera technique.

The difference between action series and comedy series is well documented. Action series, because of their debt to the Hollywood film, are more likely to use violence and as a result have been severely criticized. The situation comedy is quite a different genre: It is similar to the daytime serial (soap opera) in that only a few sets are used, and the same set is used each week; this is important for keeping costs relatively low. It is also similar to a theater play because of the live audience. There is one great difference between the daytime soap opera and the series: In the series few actors are employed, while the casts of soaps are large. In addition, the stars of Hollywood series are important persons in the production. In the daytime soap opera, when a "regular" wants to leave the show or if the producers no longer want the actor, the part is written out of the story. It is rare for even supporting actors to leave a prime-time series, although it does happen (both *M*A*S*H* and *Charlies' Angels* provide examples). However, a major star of a prime-time series is never replaced. If a star tires of a role, the show is dropped from the schedule. There are examples of several different actors playing the same role in a soap opera, which never happens in a prime-time situation comedy (Cantor, 1979a).

Other Forms

Of all the varying formats, the most criticized has been the action series. This criticism was carried over from the criticism of the Hollywood movies. From its inception television drama has been accused of being too violent. Nowhere have the critics been more influential in changing television than in this area. While violence has not decreased substantially, a major change has been the devaluation of the action series generally. Since the late 1960s, fewer action series are on the air. The western has virtually disappeared. Although there are some action series remaining, the situation comedy is the favored form (Robinson, 1979).

Because of the criticism of violence, several new forms of drama were introduced. One was the made-for-television movie. The movie format has many advantages for the networks that the series do not: The movies keep people from changing channels. A movie can be both a pilot film for a series as well as a profitable vehicle in its own right. The other new form of television drama introduced in the mid-seventies was the miniseries. These programs are closer to the serial in format. Most have been serialized novels (*QB VII* and *The Blue Knight*, for example). The episodes are usually broadcast on consecutive nights in one- or two-hour segments, and have the advantage of keeping people tuned to one station for several nights running. More important, if a miniseries has too much violence for the critics, it is easier to defend on an artistic basis or on the basis of its short run. Both movies and miniseries are suitable for reruns and syndication and, in fact, several miniseries have been produced directly for syndication, giving producers and artists less profit but more freedom than they normally have when producing directly for network distribution. Although the number of hours devoted to drama has changed little since 1968, the number of episodic series and especially the number of action series have decreased. These changes, I contend, are not due to audience choice, but rather to pressure from critics.

CULTURAL AND SOCIOLOGICAL CONTENT

Although television drama is widely viewed and criticized, it is rarely taken seriously as either a cultural or artistic form. Most of what is known about the content of television drama comes from content analyses. These analyses are usually conducted from what Paul Hirsch (1978b) calls a social problems approach and have focused on such areas of inquiry as televised violence; sexual intimacy; sex-role, occupational, and minority stereotyping; and drug or alcohol use. The usual purpose of content analyses is to provide concrete evidence to show the number of negative portrayals and images. The rationale behind these investigations is that television, considered a dynamic force in American society, influences attitudes and behaviors and in addition is a major socializing agent of young children.

The Cultural Indicators Project

For more than two decades, the issue of violence on television has been a matter of concern to Congress, educators, and social action groups. As part of that concern, research on the content of dramatic series was instigated in 1967 for the National Commission on the Causes and Prevention of Violence by the Annenberg School of Communication under the direction of George Gerbner. This research, called the Cultural Indicators Project, was continued under the sponsorship of the Surgeon General's Scientific Advisory Committee on Television and Social Behavior, (see Gerbner, 1972), the National Institute of Mental Health, and the American Medical Association. According to Gerbner and his associates (1978), the project was broadly based from the beginning. While violence-related findings have been widely published and disseminated, other information concerning the general patterns of life presented in television drama has also been gathered and analyzed.

Basically, the Cultural Indicators Project is a content analysis (called a message system analysis by the investigators). In the beginning of each season, drama is monitored and the "analyses provide information about the geography, demography, character profiles, and action structure of the world of television" (Gerbner et al., 1978:177). Because television drama has been systematically analyzed for over ten years, the data provide the most complete set of observations on violence, sex-role presentations, and demographic characteristics of the fictional characters in television drama.

The reports from the Cultural Indicators Project are complex and thorough. Through content analyses, the project has collected a body of data consisting of network dramatic programs transmitted in the evening prime time and network children's dramatic programs shown on weekend mornings for every season since 1967-1968. From this vast resource, only a few summary statements will be presented here. Those interested in the complete findings and the detailed methodology should consult the published and unpublished reports available.[7]

Violence in Dramatic Programming

The primary data from the Cultural Indicators Project are reported through a violence index composed of three types of measures. The measures show the extent to which violence occurred in the program samples (*prevalence*); the frequency and rate of violent episodes (*rate*); and the number of *roles* in which characters were the perpetrators of violence, its victims, or both. Prevalence is the percentage of programs containing any violence in the entire sample (one week of television each year). Rate is frequency of these acts in each program and in each half-hour. The acts themselves are called "violent episodes." Role is defined as the portrayal of characters as violents (committing violence) or victims (subjected to violence) or both. From these data the violence index is formed. Those associated with the project point out that this index is not a statistical finding, but serves to illustrate trends and to facilitate gross presentations.

Overall, this index indicates that violence has remained high since the inception of the project. However, it has fluctuated and varied through the years. After a steady, seven-year decline to a record low in 1973, the index rose to its 1976 peak and then dropped in 1977 to its second lowest point. The individual components of the index reflect this trend, showing that trends remain essentially the same whether they are measured by prevalence, rate of incidents per program, or percentage of major characters involved in violence.

During the low season 1977-1978, the prevalence of violence was only 75.5 percent compared with an average of about 80 percent. The rate of violence was a record high of 9.5 in 1976 and dropped to 6.7 episodes per hour in 1977. The same rate per play fell from its 1976 peak of 6.2 to 5.0 in 1977. Although the rate and prevalence of violence are of some interest, how the roles are portrayed on dramatic television has interested critics more.

More than six out of ten of all 3651 major characters studied from 1969 through 1977 were involved in some type of violence over the years. While almost any character can (and most do) get hurt in the world of television, killers outnumber those who are killed.

Sex Roles and Violence

Nearly seven out of ten men, compared with five out of every ten women, are involved in some violence. Although more men are involved in violence, women are more likely to be victims than violents. Approximately ten percent of the men and four percent of the women are involved in some killing. In general, more young characters get battered, but more old characters get killed. With increasing age, the male's risk of general victimization declines. For women, increasing age means increasing risks of both being hurt and being killed.

Class and Violence

Although members of all social classes are involved in violence, it is somewhat more dangerous to be a member of any but the large and indistinct middle class of characters. Clearly recognizable upper-class characters become most involved in killing. Lower-class characters are somewhat more likely to be killed. Women are less likely to be involved than men, but stand a higher chance of victimization when involved. Lower-class women are second only to lower-class men in their risks of getting killed.

Race

To be other than clearly white is similarly risky. Minorities are more likely to be victimized and less likely to be cast as killers than whites. Women fare worse, as usual, except that no nonwhite woman in the sample was involved in any killing. It should be noted here that very few nonwhite women appear in drama.

Character Type

According to Gerbner et al. (1978), the conflict of good and evil is the explicit message of popular drama. "Bad" characters are most involved in violence and killing. "Good" characters, especially women, are victims of violence rather than inflicting violence on others. "Good" males are also the most likely to commit violence as well, having the highest killer-killed ratio of all characters. Among females, the "good" woman bears the highest burden of both fatal and other kinds of victimization. By contrast, the "bad" woman is the most likely to commit both general violence and murder. To summarize: Violence is prevalent in television drama, with about 80 percent of all programs over the past decade containing one or more violent episodes. The highest incidence of violence occurs in action-type programs (crime, adventure, western drama and cartoons) and these have been a substantial component of network programming (Comstock et al., 1978).

Dramatic Demography

In the world of prime-time television drama, as in most mass media, men outnumber women about three to one. However, there are variations in different age brackets. Women actually outnumber men in the early twenties, but then their numbers fall to four or five times below the number of men in the old age categories. For example, over the past ten years the regular viewer of prime-time network drama saw a weekly average of five male and two female characters who were over 65 years of age. About one major male character per week was over 65; in constrast, it took an average of three and a half weeks of steady viewing to encounter a female in a central role who was over 65. Thus, the age distribution of females compared with males favors young girls and women under 35. Women are concentrated, with almost a third of their total numbers, in the 25 to 35 age bracket; one-third of the men are concentrated in the 35 to 44 age bracket. The character population is structured to provide a relative abundance of younger women and older men (Gerbner et al., 1979).

Overall, the data from the Cultural Indicators Project show that sex, age, and occupations in prime-time series add up to a complex demography. In the case of the characters analyzed, three-quarters are male, American, middle and upper class, unmarried, and in the prime of life. Women typically represent romantic or family interests, close human contact, and love. Males can act in far more occupational roles than women. Moreover, it is rare to have a female part that does not involve at least the suggestion of sexuality. Male-female differences in employment and marital status are striking: more than half of the females are married, while less than one-third of the males are. Almost two-thirds of the major female characters have no discernible paid occupation. Women are not usually found in adventure situations. An outstanding finding is that most of the time women are the leading characters in situation comedies, while men dominate the action/adventure series and programs showing high-status occupations such as law and medicine.

The world of television as reported by the Cultural Indicators Project emphasizes males, professionals, whites, and the middle class.

Although there has been an increase of blacks, blacks and whites are not shown as equal on prime-time television. Men and women are not equal in prime-time drama either: Men appear more often, have more dominant roles; women tend to be more youthful, are typically objects of sexual desires, or are emotionally supportive of the man's risk-taking (Comstock et al., 1978).

The findings from the Cultural Indicators Project are similar to those of other investigators using a similar methodology. For example, John Seggar and Penny Wheeler (1973), who analyzed formal occupational roles in 250 half-hour segments of daytime and nighttime television, found that 82 percent of these were portrayed by males. Majority (white) men were in higher-status occupational roles than were minority men. Lemon (1978) coded action shows and situation comedies and found 471 white men, 192 white women, 140 black men, and 37 black women. Every content analysis of dramatic programming yields similar results (Head, 1954; DeFleur, 1964).

Sex on Prime-Time Drama

Although critics of prime-time drama have expressed concern about sex as well as violence (see Cater and Strickland, 1975), those doing content analysis have ignored the sexual content until recently. The data that exist on the subject are recent and incomplete. Studies by Baran (1976a, 1976b) show that acts which occur frequently are kissing, embracing, flirting, nonaggressive touching, and partner-seeking. They uncovered no instance of homosexual activity and only two acts of implied or explicit heterosexual intercourse in the 50 hours they analyzed. Fernandez-Callado and Greenberg (1977, 1978) report that intimate sexual behaviors on television are usually mutually agreed-upon acts between heterosexual partners. Deviance, in the forms of homosexuality and rape, occurs infrequently; only five rapes were reported in 58 hours of television. From another similar analysis (Franzblau et al., 1977) of 61 hours of prime-time programs during the 1975-1976 season it was found that the most controversial acts (intercourse, rape, and homosexual behavior) appeared rarely. Situation comedies contained more kissing, embracing, nonaggressive touching, and innuendos than any other program type. The most recent content analysis reports that sexual interactions have increased substantially in the last few years (Silverman et al., 1979).[8]

CONTENT ANALYSES—
CRITICISM AND DEFENSE

There are number of problems associated with the content analyses reported so far. Except for the data on occupational roles and the counting of men and women, quantitative content analyses usually generate disagreement in conceptualization. For example, Gerbner's Violence Index has been criticized because it neglects pscyological and verbal violence (Newcomb, 1978). Another problem is the sampling. For example, the one week of prime-time television drama used by the Cultural Indicators Project may or may not be representative of all prime-time television drama on the air during a particular season, especially the more recent seasons. Television drama on the air in the fall may be quite different from another sample week because of the prevalence of the miniseries and movies which vary weekly in theme, plots, and characters. Also, many programs on the air in October are often dropped because of poor ratings.

Recognizing that there are problems in conceptualization, measurement, and sampling, the results of these analyses still provide the most complete knowledge about the content of television drama available. While there are many things that these studies cannot tell us, there are other things that the method can reveal but are ignored in these reports. Because the data emphasize the violent context, these studies have limited value. Also, the way the data are reported is problematic. The similarities among television plays rather than the differences in style, format, and nuances of plot are emphasized. Because the data are usually aggregated over the years, change is deemphasized although not entirely ignored. Gerbner defends his method and collection of data by explaining that his "main interest is the commonalities of exposure and association that cultivate public inceptions, rather than in the variety of individual differences" (Gerbner and Gross, 1979:223). The basic rationale for conducting the content analyses is to find out what collective lessons are presented in television drama.

Gerbner (1972:29) takes the position that drama on television serves a symbolic function. He notes that the fictional world is often very different from the real world and that dramatic behavior bears little resemblance to everyday action. The way people are presented in the drama performs the symbolic function of presenting power relationships in a way that contributes to the maintenance of power in the society. Thus, the collective lesson taught by television is to cultivate a sense of hierarchical values and forces. In the world of television drama, men are more powerful than women, whites more powerful than blacks, young women more powerful than older women in sexual encounters. Although these representations reflect some part of social reality, they are presented through fiction, not realism. The television world, for example, is much more violent than the real world. These fictional representations are presented as myths and provide cultural indicators on the state of society. Moreover, because the major function of television drama is to reproduce society through the repetition of fictional symbols and representations, drama operates as a means of social control. The product, according to Gerbner, is standardized, viewed nonselectively by most viewers, and thus the results of viewing are to cultivate images of social institutions and process.

Horace Newcomb (1974), one of the few who have examined television drama using literary analysis, also sees the content of television drama as reflecting cultural myths and social arrangements. However, because both his basic questions and methodology are different from Gerbner's, his conclusions are also different. Newcomb is looking for expressions of cultural and social concerns found in the drama. He also considers drama a powerful force in society, but he believes that everyone who watches television is "fully aware of the gap between their own lives and the lives of those happy fictional characters on television." People know they are watching fantasy; thus, the connection between drama and its effects are not clear-cut. Newcomb is interested in how the messages and symbols presented in the programs change consciousness. He wants to know why certain formulas continue to be popular with audiences. He accepts the content as given and does not ask the question important in this book: How does the content get there? He is not asking the questions about social control and power relationships (see Tuchman, 1974; Gitlin, 1979). His task, he claims, is to find out where the aesthetic qualities of television come from in the culture that produce them and to find out what qualities might become prevalent in the future (Newcomb, 1974: 24). Essentially, he sees the content as reflecting society, but he differs from Gerbner in that he sees the content as reflecting more elemental arrangements and more general societal values. For instance, he notes that Mary Tyler Moore and her fellow workers symbolized a family and believes this reflects changes in work and family relationships in the larger society. He presents a qualitative analysis of the formulas and plots and looks for deeper meanings that are attached to the larger social order. He does not deny the prevalence of violence on television, but insists that it is not possible to discuss violence without recognizing the aesthetic structure (social context) in which the violence occurs. (1974: 263).

Both Gerbner and Newcomb are basically interested in the impact of content on viewers. Because their questions and the technique they use for analysis are different, they come up with different but complementary results. Gerbner's approach to the study of content is through systematic content analysis. He also has done these quantitative studies over a period of ten years. Newcomb's technique for studying the content is through qualitative literary analysis. The two techniques, according to Hirsch (1978b), are in opposition to each other. Content analysis usually takes sequences, characters, and events as the unit of analysis and deliberately aggregates these into sum totals, outside the context of the plots and themes in which they are embedded. Literary analysts suggest this ignores and downplays the fact that these actions are highly stylized. Most literary analysts are concerned with meaning and consciousness and make the general assumption that although the plots are stereotypic and unrealistic, they engage viewers' fantasies rather than shape their images and conceptions of situations, groups, and occupations.

Another criticism of traditional content analyses is not in the methodology, but in how the methodology has been used. It is possible to use the same techniques and ask different questions. From the information available presently it is difficult to show many changes in content. The available data as they have been presented now emphasize the continuing patterns. However, as most viewers know, television drama has changed since 1954. In the last half-decade, programs which show unmarried couples living together, divorced women raising children, and single women with serious careers in drama represent changes that were considered taboo on television a generation ago. The success of *All in the Family, Roots* and other programs shows that political topics once forbidden on television are now allowed. Michael Robinson (1979), in an unsystematic review of the situation comedies, suggests that the situation comedy may be as important to sociology as it is to the networks. He says that situation comedies sell social values (Gerbner would agree). He goes on to note that in 1956 only two of the top ten shows were situation comedies: *I Love Lucy* and *December Bride.* In 1966 there were six situation comedies in the top ten and in 1978-1979 there were eight. Content analysis, as with all research methodologies, is simply a tool. The research question and problems of conceptualization are important. To find out about change, content analyses must be done over time. In that respect, the Cultural Indicators Project is exemplary. However, if one is to find out about changing themes, plots, and social relationships, then one must systematically analyze the programs for these elements. Except for the unpublished analysis by Lynda Glennon and Richard Butsch (1978), a search has only generated literary analyses relating to the issues of social values found in television drama.

Glennon and Butsch are presently analyzing social class differences in television family series. As part of this work they reported on all working-class family series appearing on prime-time network television from 1947 to 1977. This analysis reveals two recurring themes. The first, predominant from 1949 to 1966, was the characterization of the working-class husband-father as the bumbling fool. The second theme, predominant since 1971, characterizes the children of working-class families as upwardly mobile. (There were no working-class family series on the air from 1966 to 1971.) Whenever a working-class family has been given dignity, this dignity has been associated with themes of upward mobility.

Glennon and Butsch assert that in an era when male dominance was taken for granted, television consistently reversed this order when depicting the working class. According to them, during the 1960s very few (if any) middle-class programs portrayed the man as a fool and the woman as his superior. More typically, when this comedic formula was presented, the husband was intelligent, strong, and mature and the wife was the fool. For example, the dumb or childlike wife appears in *Burns and Allen*, *I married Joan*, *Wendy and Me* and *Green Acres*.

Although the documentation for change in dramatic content is weak, nonetheless changes have occurred that cannot be ignored. These changes may not be in the direction desired by the critics. Those symbols critics define as negative are still found in television drama. In a recent review of the content of television drama, the Report of the United States Commission on Civil Rights (1979) found that sex-role and minority stereotyping continues, as well as violence and crime. However, as new formats are adopted, changes also occur. There is no question that with the popularity of the situation comedy and the evening soap operas such as *Dallas* and *Soap* sexual content is more prevalent.

The question is whether values or basic ideology about sex, violence, power, and social relationships have changed. According to Gerbner et al. (1977, 1978, 1979) the changes in values are minimal. The content reflects traditional power relationships, and the only changes, as might b e expected, are cosmetic rather than basic. The difficulty with dismissing all change as cosmetic is that subtle changes become lost in the analysis.

Because content and literary analyses are conducted without considering the production process, the information they generate has limited value. Does the content reflect social changes in the society, or does it lead change? Robinson (1979) believes the latter and suggests that content reflects the values of the creators (writers and producers), which are different from those of the audience. Others think changes in content follow social change. The questions relating to change must be answered, not only through content analysis, but also by combining content analysis with a contextual analysis of how the drama is produced and selected.

If the messages are as negative as some critics suggest, it seems logical to ask who is responsible. Gerbner simply ignores the production process by saying that the creators have few degrees of freedom and that content is mass produced. There is no question that further work is necessary to better understand the content of drama. In the remainder of this book, the focus is on how the content is produced and on the controls and constraints on the creators and disseminators of drama. Television drama is not being presented as a social problem, but rather as both a form of culture and as an economic commodity.

NOTES

1. Prime-time varies in different sections of the United States. In the midwest and Rocky Mountain states, prime-time is from 7:00 p.m. to 10:00 p.m., rather than from 8:00 p.m. to 11:00 p.m. as in the eastern and far western sections of the country.

2. Action and adventure series are usually filmed; situation comedies usually videotaped. Advances in technology are making the differences in the means of capturing images minimal. It is possible to use a video camera with the same precision formerly possible only with film cameras.

3. For example, Hallmark sponsors a dramatic production written especially for television in the anthology tradition at least once a year near Christmas.

4. Most sponsors delegated authority to advertising agencies. In most agencies there were people who could be considered producers. Barnouw (1978) details the relationship among the sponsor, the agencies, and the network.

5. *Philco Television Playhouse* and *Goodyear Television Playhouse* were produced by the same advertising agency and were on the air on alternate weeks in the same time slot.

6. The 1954 show is a different series from the one presently on the air being broadcast by NBC. The title of the present show is *The Wonderful World of Disney* (Terrace, 1976b).

7. Many of the articles reporting data from the Cultural Indicators Project are cited in the bibliography. Those readers interested in the detailed reports (at least ten are available) should contact The Cultural Indicators Project, Annenberg School of Communications, University of Pennsylvania, Philadelphia, Pennsylvania.

8. Silverman et al. (1979) report that most physical suggestiveness and sexual innuendos were presented on humorous programs, namely situation comedies. Overt sexual behavior remained low in all programming.

3

LEGAL CONTEXT AND CONTROL

Relationship of broadcast industry to rules and regulations regarding free speech and legal controls as applied to television drama. Background of broadcast regulation. First Amendment and Fairness Doctrine; citizen groups, social scientists, educators, and the government; government agencies as pressure groups.

INTRODUCTION

The present state of control (and lack of control) over dramatic television content has emerged as a result of two dominant influences: application of the Communications Act of 1934 and the courts' interpretation of the First Amendment.[1] The interaction between government and broadcasting is very complex, involving technical, programming, and commercial concerns. For prime-time drama, the most important concerns are the intersecting issues of free speech and censorship. Because drama is broadcast through commercial television, monopolistic control is another important concern. The relationship between monopolistic control and free speech is problematic, revolving around the dual issues of citizens' rights of access to the airways and broadcasters' rights to control content.

The model of communications presented by many observers is a free enterprise system, existing at the pleasure of the government, yet still autonomous (see Steinberg, 1970, as an example). Stuart Hall (1974) has argued that the study of specific influences is inadequate for examining the relationship between government and broadcasting. Hall suggests that investigators should seek mutual adjustments, reciprocity of interests, and definitions derived from law as well as those developed informally between broadcasters and government agencies.

Although freedom of speech is assumed to be a legal right, the issues involved in ensuring free speech are complicated; the government is seen by some as external to broadcasting, by others as brodcasting's protector. Through the Communications Act of 1934 (Federal Communications Commission, 1971) the government is directly responsible for the organization and regulation of the broadcast industry. Moreover, the laws are both written and interpreted within the context of the larger political process. Public interest groups, content creators, business interests, and broadcasters use the legislative process, the courts, and the regulatory agencies to influence and control the content of television drama.

Since television's beginning as a national mass medium there has been a struggle over the control of prime-time drama (Cantor, 1979b). Participants in the battle pressure Congress, the Federal Communications Commission (FCC, the primary regulatory agency for broadcasting), and other agencies as well to change or gain control over broadcasting. Although the struggle over content is known to involve broadcast organizations (the three networks, local stations, sponsors), content creators (the program suppliers), and citizen groups, the role of several government agencies in this conflict is poorly understood. The government is not monolithic: two agencies can often conflict over both goals and interpretation of the law. Furthermore, government agencies can act as pressure groups in various ways, attempting to influence broadcasters by setting priorities for research and by actually trying to change content. Because the content of prime-time drama is believed to be influential in shaping attitudes and behavior, social scientists and educators have also advocated direct governmental intervention in determining prime-time content.

In this chapter, issues relating the organization of the broadcast industry to the rules and regulations concerning free speech and drama will be discussed. What follows here is a *selective* discussion; it is impossible to examine completely the myriad of laws and rulings applicable to broadcasting. Additional attention to the relevant rulings and actions—in particular, various antitrust suits against the television networks and other media organizations—is provided in Chapter 4.

BACKGROUND OF BROADCAST REGULATIONS

The broadcast industry arrived at its present basic structure—a nationwide system based on advertising revenue—in 1927, with networks linked by telephone system; local stations on temporary renewable licenses; and a regulatory commission directed to base its decisions on the public interest, convenience, and necessity. The development of national radio networks (and later television networks) as commercial enterprises was supported by laws and regulations (Barnouw, 1977).

In 1934, when the revised Communications Act was passed, the Federal Communications Commission (FCC) was established, superceding the Federal Radio Commission. In the Communications Act of 1934, radio is used as a generic term to describe both audio and visual broadcasting (Federal Communications Commission, 1971). The Communications Act clearly states the major areas of regulation vested in the FCC: issuance of licenses to local broadcasters and regulation of both old and new technologies. Section 326 of this act forbids the FCC to regulate program content. Because program content is supposedly outside the FCC jurisdiction, the networks have essentially been free from any regulatory controls. By law, a network is not considered a broadcaster; rather, networks rent air time from local stations, which broadcast the programs transmitted, usually over telephone cable from a central national location.

The relationship between the FCC and the broadcast industry has been complicated by the fact that the regulation of broadcasting is to a large degree a product of its history. Radio and television have been largely private activities and government control has been limited. More often than not, those who are supposedly regulated impose their will on the regulator (Schiller, 1969). Erwin G. Krasnow and Lawrence Longly (1973:31-33) characterize regulation as a two-way process in which the regulatory agency and those being regulated attempt to control each other. Noting that the FCC is largely dependent for much of its information about proposed policy on industry trade associations, informal discussions at meetings, and overt pressure from broadcasters, Krasnow and Longly contend that the pattern of industry-FCC relationships is dynamic, changing constantly with the shifting degrees of industry control.

Until the mid-1960s, the regulatory process was dominated by three major participants: Congress, the FCC, and the industry itself. The

National Association of Broadcasters (NAB), which comprises the three networks and approximately 4000 member radio and television stations, is the major lobbyist for the industry. Krasnow and Longley (1973) argue that in the early years of broadcasting the NAB was successful in thwarting efforts to place regulations on broadcasters that did not meet with industry approval. In recent years, however, the NAB has encountered increasing difficulty in its efforts to fend off congressional and FCC regulation. The NAB is essentially controlled by three networks, because 85 percent of all local stations are network-affiliated. Both the networks and the local stations adhere to the NAB Code, which works essentially as a mechanism of self-regulation.

The major change in the dynamics of regulation since the 1960s is due to a new participant in the regulatory process—citizen groups. Until 1966, only those with demonstrable economic clout were permitted to intervene in radio and television licensing proceedings. In 1966, the United States Court of Appeals allowed the Office of Communication of the United Church of Christ to file a petition with the FCC to deny the renewal of the licence held by WLBT-TV in Jackson, Mississippi. The challenge was made on the grounds that the station discriminated against black viewers, who constituted 45 percent of Jackson's population. This case, although involving only a local station, generated many other license challenges and protests against broadcasters relevant to the content of prime-time drama. Later in this chapter the role of community groups in relation to the content of drama will be made explicit.

Although the influence of citizen groups has had some effect, networks still enjoy a favored status in the regulatory process. In particular, the content of entertainment and drama transmitted by the networks is favored over other kinds of content. As far as regulation is concerned, television entertainment programming has been treated differently from news and public affairs programming. Drama has had an ambivalent position in the industry because most drama has been created by outside suppliers, advertising agencies in the early days of television, and later the Hollywood program suppliers associated with the movie industry. Moreover, local stations rarely, if ever, produce drama. Although legal restrictions on the networks have increased in recent years, such restriction is still limited. The FCC can regulate the television networks only indirectly, by commenting on the practices of the stations owned and operated by networks,[2] and by limiting the contractual agreements and time allotments that can be rented from the local stations (Head, 1976:305-306).

Because of the power of the networks over their affiliates, there has been concern over centralized control of television content. Since 1963, there have been several attempts to achieve a more equitable balance of power between the networks and the local stations. Prior to 1963, the standard affiliate contracts gave the networks the option on certain hours of station time each day. This practice is now prohibited by the FCC. Also by FCC regulation, network-affiliate contracts are limited to cover a period of not more than two years. At the end of this period, either the network or the station may renew or make other arrangements.

Prime Time Access Rule

In recent years, the Prime Time Access Rule has been the FCC's most important constraint on the networks. This regulation took local stations off the network during the prime-time half-hour, 7:30 to 8:00 p.m. The Prime Time Access Rule was established in answer to critics' claims that local station autonomy had been superceded by the networks. By designating one half-hour of prime time to the local stations, the FCC was attempting to encourage local public service broadcasting in place of network-contracted dramatic shows, usually an episodic series. What actually happened was quite different from what the FCC and the critics desired. In most parts of the country, the 7:30-8:00 p.m. time period has been filled with game shows or syndicated film programs similar to the dramatic shows they replaced. Although more locally produced programs have been aired in this time period in some parts of the country, more commonly the shows on the air have been produced elsewhere and purchased from a syndication company. This outcome is explained by noting how costly it is for local stations to produce half-hour programs five times each week (Head, 1976:390-394).

Family Viewing Hour

In addition to the Prime Time Access Rule, the hours between 7:00 and 9:00 p.m. have been designated Family Viewing Hours, during which no dramatic programs with "adult" content may be shown. Adult content refers to those programs containing violence or sex. This designation was not an overt requirement of the FCC; Family Viewing

Time evolved through an agreement between the FCC and the networks because of the continuous and ever-increasing criticism from citizen groups, social scientists, and educators about the content of dramatic shows. The plan developed during the winter of 1974, when network executives, FCC staff, and their respective lawyers met. According to this plan, the networks agreed to keep the evening hours from 7:00 to 9:00 free of themes that might be objectionable for child viewers. Since the first half-hour is generally filled by network and local news and the second half-hour was already taken from the networks by the Prime Time Access Rule, in reality only 60 minutes (from 8:00 to 9:00 p.m.), became known as the "Family Hour." Arthur E. Taylor, then president of CBS Television, was the chief proponent of the plan. Under Taylor's leadership, the plan was adopted into the NAB code in April 1975 and became policy at the start of the 1975-1976 season.

This was the first attempt to publicly control television drama. In November 1976, the Federal District Court in Los Angeles declared the Family Viewing Hour unconstitutional. The plaintiffs in this suit were the Writers' Guild of America, the Screen Actors' Guild, the Directors' Guild, and several production companies (Writers Guild, West v. FCC, 1976). The defendants argued that the code revision was merely an attempt at self-regulation, similar to codes of ethics issued by other industries and professions. The plaintiffs argued that the FCC had coerced the networks into establishing the Family Viewing Hour. The judge ruled that although self-regulation may be desirable, it must be true self-regulation, not a kind of restriction imposed or threatened by the government. If the government intimidates, then the self-regulation in matters of expression is unconstitutional. Essentially, the court stated that the broadcasters' action in adopting the Family Viewing Hour violated the First Amendment rights of those who were creating the drama. As of this writing, the Family Viewing Hour is still in effect because the Los Angeles Court's decision is being appealed by the three networks (Brief for Appellants, 1977).

THE FIRST AMENDMENT AND FAIRNESS

Although some regulations directly apply to the scheduling and time alloted to prime-time drama transmitted by the networks, prime-time drama is still freer and more autonomous from regulation and outside censorship than news and public affairs programs. Drama exists in its present form because of the way the First Amendment has been interpreted by the courts, because Congress and the FCC have supported the networks' definition of free speech, and because of the ways antitrust laws have been applied. There has been an increased effort to regulate news programs since 1964, when the Fairness Doctrine, adopted by the FCC in 1949, was rewritten. The Fairness Doctrine states in part that broadcasters "must afford reasonable opportunity for the presentation of contrasting viewpoints on controversial issues of public importance" (Federal Register, 1974). Some see this doctrine as a direct contradiction of Section 326 of the Communications Act of 1934, which states in part:

> Nothing in this Act shall be understood or construed to give the Commission (FCC) the power of censorship over radio. . . . [N]o regulation or condition shall be fixed by the Commission which shall interfere with the right of free speech by means of radio communication.

In 1969, the Supreme Court, responding to the Red Lion Broadcasting Company's challenge of this doctrine, held that the rights of the audience, not the rights of broadcasters, are paramount in the fairness doctrine. In this decision the Fairness Doctrine has been specifically interpreted to mean that stations and even the television networks are obligated to carry out the letter of the doctrine and "to afford reasonable opportunity for discussing conflicting views on issues of public importance" (Red Lion v. FCC, 1969). Moreover, the Supreme Court held that the Fairness Doctrine does not violate the First Amendment rights of the broadcaster, but only ensures protection of the rights of the audience.

This decision, however, has been interpreted to mean that only news or public or personal attacks on an individual are considered issues of public importance. Regardless of the issues discussed in drama, the Fairness Doctrine does not apply (Friendly, 1975). Dramatic teleplays, regardless of the subject matter, are free from the governmental control associated with the Fairness Doctrine, while news and public affairs are controlled both through the Supreme Court's interpretation of the First Amendment and the FCC's decisions in individual cases.

Both the FCC's application of the Fairness Doctrine to news programs only and the Red Lion decision have generated public debate. The debate, much simplified, is between those who believe that the First Amendment guarantees a free marketplace of ideas in which citizens are exposed to a wide diversity of views and opinions on important issues, and those who hold to a more narrow interpretation of the First Amendment (Head, 1976:321-328). If the letter of the amendment is strictly observed, then those who write, create, or produce television should be free to express ideas and points of view without interference from government, other agencies, and individuals. Logically, these two perspectives are not mutually exclusive; in fact, they might be interpreted as mutually supportive. Nevertheless, those who hold that the First Amendment guarantees a free marketplace of ideas are usually outside of the industry, often trying to make the media more responsive to minority group opinion. Those holding the view that the media should be free from any and all control include both strict civil libertarians and the media people who own, write, and create the programs.

Those who adhere to the free marketplace interpretation of the First Amendment are usually concerned with two separate but related processes: the monopolistic or oligopolistic concentration of control which reduces the diversity of communication, and the "unfair" practices that distort or selectively screen those materials that are aired. According to Sidney Head (1976:398-400), the FCC and the courts have sought to interpose the First Amendment as a protection against the restraints which have emerged because so few people are involved in the selection of news and public affairs programming. Civil libertarians and media people maintain an opposite view: that government should never interfere in freedom of expression or in business practices related to freedom of expression.

The debate is further complicated because a distinction is made between entertainment and news programs. Congress and the broadcasting industry have historically supported the view that dramatic television should be free from all governmental controls. Citizen groups, especially those concerned with violence and its effects on children, as well as some educators and social scientists disagree. These groups see drama as an issue of public importance; they take the position that drama shapes attitudes and is thus a primary means of socializing the young.

Congress, Violence, and the First Amendment

The FCC's power to regulate broadcasting comes from Congress, which established the Commission in 1934 as part of the Communications Act (Barnouw, 1977). Congressional committees oversee both the FCC and the broadcasting industry. In the House of Representatives, the relevant committee is the Interstate and Foreign Commerce Committee; in the Senate, the Interstate Commerce Committee. From its beginning, television has been the object of concern to both Congress and to various citizen groups. Much of the early and continuing concern has been directed to the effects of television drama on children. Since 1954, when Senator Estes Kefauver, Chairman of the Subcommittee on Juvenile Delinquency, conducted the first investigation focusing on crime, sex, and violence in programming content, there have been over ten subsequent investigations or hearings on this subject. Some of these investigations have led to research; others have resulted in proposed changes in the Communications Act. The most important function of these hearings has been to allow various dissident groups a chance to talk directly to lawmakers and the networks, providing a context for open debate.

Criticism of television has been so extensive that it is impossible to discuss all the concerns of various segments of the population. For example, because of the assassinations and riots during the mid-1960s, President Lyndon Johnson appointed the National Commission on the Causes and Prevention of Violence. This commission set up a task force on the media. While warning of the danger of making television a "scapegoat," the commission issued a strong statement on violence, recommending that violence be reduced in all programming (and especially dramatic programs) and that significant research be conducted on the subject (Cater and Strickland, 1975:12; Eisenhower, 1969).

In 1955, John Pastore became chairman of the Senate Subcommittee on Communications of the Interstate Commerce Committee. The television quiz scandals of 1958-1959 (see Chapter 4; Barnouw, 1978; Melody, 1973) prompted Pastore's first look at industry practices. Network officials were engaged in public hearings and this subjected them to informal pressures that Pastore and the committee hoped would result in self-regulation. In this way, Congress could be involved in public debate without engaging in formal action which might be interpreted as trespassing on the First Amendment (Cater and Strictland, 1975:15).

Because of the public concern about violence and the suggestions of the Violence Commission, Senator Pastore's committee recommended that research be conducted into the potential relationship between sex and violence on television and antisocial behavior among young people. A million-dollar research project was funded, resulting in the so-called Surgeon General's Report on television and violence (Surgeon General's Scientific Advisory Committee on Television and Social Behavior, 1972).[3] The study was fraught with controversy, but its results convinced both public action groups and some social scientists that, according to current regulation, the interests of children were less significant than civil libertarian interpretations of the First Amendment. In particular, Action for Children's Television and the Parent-Teacher Association pressured the networks, the FCC, and Congress for greater governmental involvement in programming. The networks responded to this pressure by initiating the Family Viewing Hour.

Few, including Senator Pastore, conceptualized the relevant issues in terms of the Fairness Doctrine. Fred Friendly (1975) notes that Senator Pastore recognized the paradoxes and inconsistencies in the interpretation of the First Amendment. Pastore, in an interview reported by Friendly, agreed that the Fairness Doctrine should apply only to news and public affairs programs, not dramatic shows. The interviewer mentioned a number of specific controversial issues discussed in drama in recent years. For example, *Maude* has presented a series episode on birth control; an episode of *The Mary Tyler Moore Show* discussed reporters' shield laws; and numerous movies made for television and miniseries have had political themes (the Cuban missile crisis, John Dean's *Blind Ambition*, John Ehrlichman's novel *The Company*, *Roots*, and many others). Pastore was asked: "Doesn't it seem inconsistent to you that the FCC will tell the documentary and news people what fairness is and how to correct it, but don't do so to the producers of Archie Bunker, or on a re-enactment of the missile crisis?" "That would be censorship," he responded (Friendly, 1975:202). Friendly reports that Pastore's reasoning was based on the fact that because there is such a large number of entertainment shows, the content of a particular program tends to be balanced by other, similar programs presenting a different point of view. Many social scientists and critics, however, do not agree with the view that the content of drama is diverse and varied.

Citizen Groups and the First Amendment

Citizen groups such as the United Church of Christ, the National Organization for Women (NOW), Action for Children's Television, and the Parent-Teacher Association have expressed concern about the messages contained in television drama. Their response to the content of drama (and other issues related to broadcasting) is multifaceted. One common response has been to use FCC procedures for citizen participation in the regulation of broadcasting. Thus, many groups have petitioned the FCC to deny the renewal of local stations' licenses.

By regulation, every broadcasting station in the United States must reapply every three years for the privilege of broadcasting over the public airways. Because of the court action involving WLBT-TV in Jackson, Mississippi, there has been a proliferation of petitions from citizen groups to deny licenses in recent years. Changes in the FCC definition of fairness, the Supreme Court's 1969 decision to revoke the WLBT-TV license, and the FCC regulations forbidding local stations to discriminate in employment have all contributed to the new militancy of social action groups in the early 1970s. Moreover, almost no VHF channels were available to minority or other citizen groups. Using the lack of easy access as one argument for their petitions, these citizen groups translated their social concerns into social action.

Although the Fairness Doctrine and discrimination in employment rulings apply only to local stations and not to the networks and program suppliers, citizen groups have used the license challenge as one means to protest what they consider negative portrayals in drama. Most license challenges consider three aspects of FCC regulations: The Fairness Doctrine; Equal Employment Opportunities; and ascertainment of community needs, which is required of all stations. Because both equal employment and ascertainment are clearly local issues, they are not immediately relevant to the discussion here. However, the Fairness Doctrine *is* relevant: Several citizen groups have interpreted the Fairness Doctrine to include all program content, including drama.

One license challenge (the WRC-TV petition) in particular generated opinions and court decisions which led to the Reports of the United States Commission on Civil Rights (1977, 1979). This challenge also may have been partially instrumental in generating an FCC investigation of network practices now in progress (Howard, 1979). In 1972, NOW challenged the license of WRC-TV, the NBC-owned station in Washington, D.C. Although lawyers and others involved in drafting the brief to deny the WRC-TV license were aware that the station did not produce the prime-time drama transmitted locally, they nonetheless decided to include the content of drama along with other content in their definition of fairness. As part of their petition, they argued that women were not fairly represented in drama because they were underrepresented compared with male characters and because they were not shown in a variety of roles and occupations. They argued that the employment of women and women's changing roles in society were issues of public importance; therefore, the Fairness Doctrine should apply to drama. The content of drama was found to be so biased that differing points of view about women were not available. This, according to NOW, produced a negative effect on girls and women because they were deprived of appropriate role models (NOW, 1972).

The FCC's response to the petition was that the First Amendment and Section 326 of the Communications Act did not allow any action regarding the portrayal of women, in television programming. As expected, WRC-TV's license was renewed. However, in a separate opinion, FCC Commissioner Benjamin Hook suggested that the FCC did have jurisdiction to review the status of women in television programs. The United States Court of Appeals, in a subsequent review of the FCC's decision to renew WRC-TV's license, drew on Commissioner Hook's suggestion that the FCC might conduct an overall inquiry into the subject. Although the court did not order such an inquiry, it made clear that such an undertaking was within the authority of the FCC.

The effectiveness of citizen groups in changing broadcasting has been questioned. Because local stations are clearly responsible to Equal Employment Opportunity regulations at the station level, citizen groups may have had more impact in the area of employment practices than in programming (Hanks and Pickett 1979). Although activist groups have successfully used the law to reach agreements with several local stations about a number of issues, the only control local stations can exercise over dramatic programs is to refuse to broadcast them. This is rarely done. The law may be vague about the responsibility for program content, but it is clear that the production companies supplying the drama are completely free from both employment and content regulations. The 1952 Supreme Court decision guarantees freedom of speech to the movie industry (Schumach, 1964). This reversed the ruling that had stood since 1915, which asserted that the movie industry was simply a business. Of course, the program suppliers are subject to the same pressures as the local stations and the networks, but this pressure has no legal underpinnings (*TV Guide*, 1977).

SOCIAL SCIENTISTS AND EDUCATORS

Many social scientists and educators consider the sociological subject matter of television drama to be a matter of major consequence. Social scientists have been studying the way the sexes are portrayed, the violence, and the dramatic demography, including the ratio of men to women and the occupational roles assigned to different classes, groups, and sexes. The consequences, particularly to children, of viewing both violence and stereotypic portrayals are considered by many to be detrimental to human development. While most people assume that the motives of those who protest the content of television drama are unselfish and well-intentioned, the strict libertarians believe these critics constitute a threat to the future of freedom of speech (Seiden, 1974:137). Many social scientists and others espouse mental health for children and adults, racial and sexual equality, increased educational programming, and improvements in the quality of dramatic offerings, as well as reduced violence. Yet, regardless of the orientation of such groups, their actions could well result in increased control, according to those who oppose their actions. For example, David Hamblin of the Illinois Civil Liberties Union has argued that any government attempt to limit the amount of violence on television would be an abridgement of the First Amendment (Phillips, 1977).

Social scientists who advocate more government intervention in the content of television do not perceive the issue in First Amendment terms. They are most interested in the negative effects on children or in the general functions of the media in society. Robert Liebert and his associates (1973:157), after reviewing the Surgeon General's Report and related literature, conclude: "The demonstrated teaching and instigating effects of aggressive television fare upon youth are of sufficient importance to warrant immediate remedial action." One remedy Liebert recommends is more government control over television. He suggests that Congress should be convinced that violence is indeed injurious. One solution is to change the law so that the networks would be licensed in the same way the broadcast stations are licensed. He expects no First Amendment problems, because violence is "intrinsically injurious." (Obscenity has usually been considered intrinsically injurious). The problem would be solved for Liebert if Congress and the courts could be convinced that violence was as damaging as obscenity (Liebert et al., 1973:167-68).

Douglass Cater and Stephen Strickland (1975) also have been very critical of the government and the networks regarding the issue of television violence. They conclude their book on television and the child with a quotation from Meredith Wilson, then director of the Center for Advanced Study in the Behavioral Sciences at Stanford: "In my judgment, violence is clearly dangerous enough to be called to the attention of Congress, the industry and the public. It merits attention and it requires constructive action" (Cater and Strickland, 1975:139). Cater and Strickland do not examine the various interpretations of the First Amendment and pay only lip-service to its preservation, briefly noting that the First Amendment of the Constitution should operate as a strong restraint in the area of lawmaking.

Other social scientists express broader concerns over television content. Several writers recognize that the issues are political and economic. Herbert Gans, for example, says "in heterogeneous societies, the struggles between diverse groups and aggregates over the allocation of resources and power are not limited strictly to economic and political issues, but also extend to cultural ones" (Gans, 1974:3). The struggle for control of cultural content, especially the control of television drama, is basically an economic issue. Gans is pessimistic about the potential for changing television content through social activism. He argues that since most mass media programs are profitable, there is little incentive to change them. Nor, according to Gans, is the government likely to act, because it lacks incentives to alter the status quo. Moreover, there is no tradition in America for using political pressure to bring about government participation in cultural creation.

GOVERNMENT AGENCIES
AS PRESSURE GROUPS

As a broad generalization, Gans' analysis may be correct, but he does not recognize the extent to which government has become involved in dramatic television in the last ten years. For example, the government has been and continues to be directly involved in the production and creation of television drama for both children and adults. Through grants and support for noncommercial and educational television there is direct government support for films and teleplays. The Corporation for Public Broadcasting,[4] the National Endowments for the Arts and Humanities, the Office of Education, and several other government agencies support or engage in dramatic production (Mielke et al., 1975). Some of these dramas are shown on commercial television. The Office of Education tries through various means to have the dramatic series made under its auspices (Emergency School Aid Act) shown through network television. Often the content of these programs, especially those made for children, can be said to be of a controversial nature, espousing such views as racial and ethnic integration.

Other agencies use different methods to influence the content of drama. The National Institute on Alcohol Abuse and Alcoholism convened an ad hoc committee of broadcasters, creators, and entertainment union people. The purpose of the meeting was to encourage those attending to present the uses of alcohol in ways which would be positive rather than negative (Ad Hoc Committee on Alcohol and the Media Meeting, 1976). Such meetings are not unusual. The Administration on Aging sponsored a similar meeting in which broadcasters and social scientists were gathered to hear the results of research on portrayals of the aged in prime-time drama. The primary purpose of this meeting was to alert network officials and others to the fact that the prime-time dramatic series neglects problems of aging and rarely shows old people on the screen (Gerbner et al., 1979).

Probably the most obvious example of a government agency acting as a pressure group is the investigation and subsequent Reports of the United States Commission on Civil Rights (1977, 1979). The Civil Rights Commission examined in detail the participation of minorities and women in television programming from the standpoint of equal economic and employment opportunities, as well as from the standpoint of how women and minorities are portrayed on the screen. The focus of the study was an in-depth look at the entire decision-making process concerning content, including the organization of the industry itself. The results of these studies were transmitted in draft to the FCC and, upon completion, to the U.S. Congress. The report made a series of recommendations concerning primetime drama which were transmitted to the FCC, the production companies, and the network programming executives. The Civil Rights Commission recommended that the FCC conduct an inquiry which would result in rule-making concerning the portrayal of minorities and women in commercial television drama. As rationale for such a recommendation, the commission cited the results of the NOW challenge discussed above. In addition, the commission reports suggested that suppliers and networks should incorporate more minorities and women into television drama. The response from both the industry and the FCC was to cite the First Amendment and Section 326 of the Communications Act.

Although the Civil Rights Commission has the legal authority to carry out its investigation, it can act only as a lobbyist or pressure group to try to ensure that its recommendations are implemented. In that regard, because the power base of the commission is limited to women and minorities who are financially weak, the success of the commission has been very limited.

CONCLUSION: FUTURE POSSIBILITIES

The solution offered most frequently to resolve the debate over control of television content is that the Communications Act of 1934 be rewritten. However, each side of the debate has a different suggestion concerning the formulation of the new law. The strict libertarians and some broadcasters suggest that television should be deregulated. Citizens, some social scientists, and other pressure groups want more regulation; in particular, they would like the networks to be regulated in the same manner as are the local stations. Because Congress was responsible for the creation of television as we know it, Congress can also pass laws to change the structure of the industry. The Public Broadcasting Act of 1967 was one result of the ongoing protest concerning television content. Public action groups' suggestions that the networks be licensed have rarely been considered seriously, although this suggestion has been made repeatedly during the last 20 years. The most recent attempt to rewrite the Communications Act emphasizes deregulation more than regulation (U.S. Congress, House, 1979). This bill proposed that the seven-member FCC be replaced by a five-member Communications Regulatory Commission with more limited power. It also would have ordered an immediate end to most federal regulation of radio broadcasters and cable operators. In about 10 years, regulation of television broadcasters would also have been lifted.

For public interest and citizen groups, the most distressing element in the bill was the proposed elimination of the Fairness Doctrine. After lobbying from both industry sources (some of whom are afraid of cable television proliferating) and public action groups, the bill was abandoned (*Wall Street Journal*, 1979). The public action groups consider it a victory to maintain the status quo. However, as Newton

Minnow (1973) has stated: "Television is not open to all, but rather it is strictly regulated by a government agency. Only a few groups may obtain broadcasting licenses, and only a limited number of programs can be broadcast by these license stations."

Anyone who has the necessary resources can make a dramatic program. However, only the three television networks can decide if and when that program will be broadcast. The local affiliates have only veto power over the decisions to show a program on the air. Thus, the law provides little regulation that directly ensures an open market place of ideas through drama.

It is doubtful that any bill such as the one introduced by Senator Strom Thurmond in January 1979 which would regulate the networks and the content directly would pass Congress (U.S. Congress, Senate, 1979). Rather than passing new laws or even amending the Communications Act, Congress has traditionally preferred to use a variety of informal techniques, such as hearings, investigations, and studies. This is not to imply that new legislation is impossible. When (or if) the wide adoption of cable, pay television, and videotape and discs breaks the control of the networks over the marketplace, the law will probably change. In the meantime, interested parties, both those with economic concerns and those with social concerns, will continue to pressure Congress and the various agencies to act in their interests.

The major struggle for control of content has taken place in the marketplace and the courts. However, the laws as they are presently written support marketplace conditions. Moreover, the Communications Act of 1934 provides support for the other institutions and organizations responsible for prime-time drama. The networks and the production companies are, practically speaking, autonomous and free from regulation. This formal autonomy is not the primary-force in shaping content; however, drama would be different if the controls and supports from the government were changed.

NOTES

1. The First Amendment to the United States Constitution states in part: "Congress shall make no law. . . . abridging the freedom of speech and the press."

2. Each network by law can own and operate five VHF television stations or seven UHF stations. At one time these stations accounted for the major profits of the networks. They are still very important to the operations of the network because in total they account for 25 percent of the possible audience in the United States. Throughout this book when discussing affiliates, the owned and operated stations will be included except when specifically mentioned separately.

3. For an excellent summary of the research see Bogart (1972). The Report was not from the Surgeon General but to the Surgeon General from the Advisory Committee on Television and Social Behavior. Because it is commonly called the Surgeon General's Report, I will also use that name throughout.

4. The Corporation for Public Broadcasting is not a government agency, but rather a quasi-government agency incorporated in the District of Columbia. It was established by the Public Broadcasting Act of 1967 as a private corporation, funded by Congress.

4

ORGANIZATIONAL CONTEXT AND CONTROL

Network power and control. How drama is produced and created. Description and analysis of the present system of production and dissemination. Television networks and their relationship to program suppliers, advertisers, local stations, and rating services.

Although television is a regulated industry in the United States, the organizations responsible for both the transmission and the creation of content have as their primary goal *profit*. There are, of course, other social functions associated with television: Television serves as a means of supplying entertainment and information to almost every household in the United States. However, entertainment and information are provided by organizations directed primarily by the profit motive, rather than to enlighten or educate viewers.[1]

Because the product of television is culture, its creation is different from other profit-making activities, such as the manufacture of material goods. The production of any commercial film drama, whether it is meant for theater distribution or for dissemination over television, can analytically be divided into two functions, those concerned with profit and those concerned with the craft aspects of creation (Moore, 1961). The craft aspects of production will be considered in the next chapter. Here the major focus will be on the business functions associated with production. However, because profit is the major determinant of the content of television drama, the profit motive is influential on craft decisions as well. Those who control access to the airways—the networks and the advertisers—set the stage for the creators, limiting their autonomy in many ways. To make a film, financial support is necessary. To have a film disseminated the filmmaker must find those who control the means of distribution. The financiers and distributors can be conceptualized as primary audiences for a film. If creators do not receive financial support, they cannot make a film. In addition, if the creators do not please the distributor, access to the ultimate audience is impossible.

Nowhere is the relationship between the creation of art (or culture) and the market economy more apparent than in the way the broadcast industry operates. Program suppliers or producers of film hire writers, directors, actors, and technicians to make films. These films are purchased by the television networks. The networks transmit the drama along with commercial advertisements through local broadcast stations which are either owned and operated by them or affiliated with them through contractual agreement. To judge whether the programs and commercials are reaching the target audience, rating services are employed who, through polling and sampling homes with mechanical devices and diary-type records, find the approximate size and composition of the audience. If a program does not reach the desired number and type of viewers, it is dropped from the schedule and another program is broadcast in its place. Production companies therefore are dependent on the networks to purchase the programs they produce and to continue to show these programs throughout a season. The networks provide the subsidies necessary to make a film and also provide the means of distributing the film. For a theater film, these two functions are separate. Because the networks finance the creation and distribution of films, they have extraordinary power in the complex processes associated with the creation of drama. Of course, the networks are dependent on the producers, the advertisers, and the local stations for their profits. Control shifts as various groups and individuals gain or lose power in the ongoing struggle over the content of television drama (Cantor, 1979b). The power of the networks was at its height in the late 1960s. Events such as government antitrust actions and citizen group pressure have contributed to a slight erosion of network power and to an increase in control from program suppliers.

Although the three networks at the present time are the most powerful influence on television drama, they too exist in a social and political context where they depend on others for profits and where outside groups want access to the airways. In Chapter 3 some of the legal and regulatory constraints were discussed. The legal system essentially supports the market operations of the networks at the present time. In this chapter the relationship among the networks, program suppliers, advertisers, and the local stations will be examined. The chapter will be divided as follows: (1) A description of the present system; (2) networks-advertisers in historical context; (3) networks and program suppliers; (4) networks, advertisers, and the ratings; and (5) the local stations and the networks.

THE PRESENT SYSTEM

A commercial television network is part of a national broadcasting system characterized by (1) competitive free advertising, (2) distribution of programs by means of a national network of stations, and (3) government regulation (as a compromise between public and private interests). The three major networks in the United States function in a similar fashion. A network sells advertising spots and programs to national advertisers and distributes programs which are either produced directly or licensed from other producers. A network has been described briefly as "a group of connected stations broadcasting the same television programs" (Spilbeck, 1960).

Due to the nature of the medium (distribution of program material and the repetitive pattern of broadcasting), the major local television stations find it desirable to affiliate with a major network. The network-affiliate relationship is contractual and controlled by government regulation (see Chapter 3). Networks can also own and operate stations, but they are limited to seven (five if VHF) by the FCC. Such stations provide income as well as production facilities for the network. Most stations are affiliated by contract, not by ownership. A local affiliated station, if it is not network-owned, legally controls what actually' appears on the air.

Although there is some variation among the networks, the organization of all three is similar: (1) *sales division* with departments for research, advertising, and promotion; (2) *distribution division* with departments of engineering, station relations, and traffic (communications networks among the stations); (3) *program division* with departments for production, production services, continuity acceptance, news, public affairs, and general programming; (4) *business division* with departments for administration, finance and accounting, labor relations, personnel, and legal matters. Headquarters for the three major networks are in New York City, and each of the networks also maintains major production and programming centers in the Los Angeles area.

The departments in the program division concerned with programming and continuity acceptance are of major interest in this book. All three networks subscribe to the Television Code of the NAB. The code has been revised several times since its adoption in 1952, but its essential character and functions are to keep governmental regulations minimal by avoiding program practices that would offend pressure groups and advertisers. Also, within the programming department there are officials who make decisions on financing and scheduling matters. Because the networks' primary function is to provide programming which will attract audiences, they presently control the production process of drama in a variety of ways: (1) The networks finance the d evelopment of story concepts, scripts and pilot films. (2) The networks decide what drama will be broadcast each season. (3) They decide when a particular show will appear during the primetime hours. (4) The networks decide whether an episodic series once on the air will be discontinued (cancelled) or whether it will continue. (5) In the name of self-regulation they apply censorship to all scripts. (6) Finally, the networks decide how much air time will be devoted to drama, variety shows, public affairs programs, specials, documentaries, and sport events. The power of the scheduling and production of drama has ramifications in Hollywood because if the networks decide to devalue drama, less work is available for the creative people.

The structure of the network system of broadcasting has changed very little since its beginnings in radio over 50 years ago (Barnouw, 1977). However, the control the networks have had over programming has changed substantially. To repeat, a television network is simply an organization which transmits programs (historically over telephone lines) to local broadcasting stations which in turn broadcast the programs to those homes reached by their assigned frequencies. Although all three networks have produced (and still are producing) some of the programs which they then transmit, their primary purpose is to supply programs to those stations they own or are affiliated with through contractual agreements. NBC, ABC, and CBS each have about 200 affiliated local stations across the United States to which they feed 12 to 14 hours of programming and commercial advertisements daily. Three of the 12 to 14 hours each day are considered primetime. These evening hours from 8:00 to 11:00 on the east and west coasts and 7:00 to 10:00 in the midwest and Rocky Mountain states attract the largest numbers of steady viewers. Thus, they are the most profitable hours for the networks. A large proportion of the prime-time hours each week is devoted to drama.

The networks pay program suppliers to produce the drama they disseminate. In addition, they pay affiliated local stations a small fee for running the shows. The networks make their profits from selling air time to the advertisers (sponsors). The sponsors in turn produce the commercial advertisements and pay the networks huge fees to show these commercials during the broadcast day. The costs to the advertisers vary according to the size of the audience. Therefore, the fees generated during the primetime hours are greater than at any other time.

The local stations are not obligated to carry network programs, but most of their revenues also come from selling their own commercials which are aired alongside those supplied by the networks (especially during the station breaks). The popularity of a network-sponsored show will also determine the fee a local station can charge for a commercial. The local stations do not have the financial resources to produce shows which will attract large audiences; therefore, they are dependent on the networks for programming. Because the advertising rates charged at both the national and local levels are determined by the ratings, both the networks and the local stations want to maximize the number of viewers. Most of the time local stations and networks have the same objectives, and both rely heavily on the rating services to help them determine the popularity of the shows and the fees charged to advertisers.

NETWORKS—ADVERTISERS—
HISTORICAL CONTEXT

Prime-time drama had its antecedents in network radio (see Chapter 2). In the 1930s, the sponsor decided on radio dramatic programming. If a sponsor decided to change a program, network assent was considered pro forma. The sponsor was assumed to hold a "franchise" on the time periods purchased directly from the networks. Many programs were created by advertising agencies and were designed to fulfill specific sponsor objectives. The director was likely to be an advertising agency staff employee. During dress rehearsal, an official of the sponsoring company was often on hand in the sponsor's booth, prepared to order last-minute changes. In NBC's headquarters and studios—Radio City in New York City, completed in 1933—every studio had a sponsor's booth (Barnouw, 1978:33).

During the decade 1945-1955, television drama was almost wholly produced live with strong theater influence. By the end of the decade network dramatic programs were almost exclusively filmed in Hollywood. Advertising agencies provided the subsidies needed to produce both live and film drama. However, the power of the sponsor in relationship to the networks was changing. The networks were not pleased with the degree of control wielded by the advertising agencies and the sponsors. William Paley, President of CBS, was determined that television should evolve differently from radio; and Sylvester L. Weaver, Jr., who became President of NBC in 1953, argued for a "magazine concept" of placing commercials. Under the magazine system, a program would not be under the control of a single sponsor, but rather sponsors would buy inserts in programs produced by the networks or by independent producers under network control. The magazine concept was not well received by the advertisers.[2]

Most sponsors continued to control programs. However, producing television drama was far more costly than radio drama, and segment sponsorship or alternate sponsorship became common during the 1950s. For example, *Philco Television Playhouse* and *Goodyear Television Playhouse* were the same series, with Philco and Goodyear alternating sponsorship each week. These arrangements involved some diffusion of control, but until the quiz scandals of 1959, sponsors essentially retained control over dramatic production. Independent producers sold their films directly to the sponsors, who in turn purchased prime airtime from the networks. *I Love Lucy*, an early film series, was sponsored entirely by the Phillip Morris cigarette company and was under its direct control. U.S. Steel sponsored a live dramatic series produced by the Theater Guild under the supervision of Batten, Barton, Durstine, and Osborn, an advertising agency. Although the live productions were considered by many to be artistically superior to the film series, the advertising agencies exercised editorial control over both. Many topics were considered taboo and were censored, especially those considered to be "liberal" or "anti-American" by the right-wing groups then pressuring the networks and advertising agencies.

The sponsor control of all prime-time programming did cause concern in the FCC. In 1959 it authorized a staff study of "television network program procurement" in which advertising agencies and others were questioned about program decision-making (Barnouw, 1978:53-54). Almost concurrently with the FCC investigation, Charles Van Doren, who had won $129,000 as a contestant on the quiz show *Twenty-One*, finally admitted after repeatedly denying any misconduct that all answers to quiz questions had been given to him in advance. His admission of perjured testimony brought forth some 100 other contestants who had appeared on several quiz shows then popular. Contestants and producers of the shows admitted they had lied to a grand jury investigating the irregularities of the quiz shows. This scandal led to congressional hearings, more FCC probes, and lawsuits. A most important consequence of these quiz show scandals was the reorganization of network operations regarding sponsorship.

This reorganization had two major effects on prime-time drama. Instead of the sponsors acting as primary censors, the networks became the only censors for the dramatic series. All scripts had to pass censor approval, and network officials often sat in on story conferences and watched series and other dramatic productions. Before 1959 the networks had offices called "broadcast standards" or "standards and practices" which applied the NAB Code to programs (see Winick, 1959), but after the quiz scandals these offices became much more powerful than they had been in the past. In addition to applying the NAB Code, the censors also applied standards concerning the use of hidden commercial advertisements within the program content. Often these commercials were accidental. In outdoor street scenes a sign advertising a particular company might inadvertently be captured on film. Since 1960 great care has been taken in seeing that such advertisements do not appear in drama. A more serious problem is displaying a commercial product during a drama, such as a bottle of whiskey on a table. These kinds of hidden commercials were the result of an agreement between producers and advertisers. In return for mentioning or showing the product, the producer was rewarded with money or a gift (often the product) in lieu of money. Network control stopped this practice. After 1959, there were incidents when the sponsor objected to some material on a show, and rarely an actual film segment for a series was made but not shown on the air because the advertiser did not approve (Cantor, 1971:64). However, because of network practices, the power of the sponsor remained, but became less direct.

The most important change came in 1960. That year four out of five dramatic shows in primetime were licensed (sold) to the networks which carried them, and in turn segments or spots were sold to the advertisers for commercials. This essentially reversed previous practice. Up until 1967, a few of the more prominent sponsors (such as Proctor and Gamble) were still making an occasional pilot film, but after 1960 these pilots often were not purchased by the networks although they had a guaranteed sponsor. By the mid-1960s the networks had gained firm control of the selection and scheduling of shows.

THE PRODUCTION COMPANIES

Although prime-time drama is broadcast on television, its production represents a marriage between the Hollywood movie and radio drama. The episodic series were originally radio with pictures (see Chapter 2). The format for television drama is partially determined by the 15-minute station break, partially by the themes and stories which were popular with radio and movie audiences, and partially by the nature of the movie industry in the United States. Decisions concerning the selection and placing of shows within the prime-time schedule are made in New York by network executives; the idea for the shows usually come from the production houses in Los Angeles. When drama moved to Los Angeles in the 1950s, independent producers rented space in the empty Hollywood studios which once hummed with feature film activities. Because film production companies in Hollywood were suffering financially, independent agencies were able to rent studio space and develop and package low-budget series, usually 13 weeks long (Seldes, 1964). However, because such programs had to attract a large audience, more money was put into their production by the larger studios. These studios (and during the 1960s the networks themselves) captured film production for television. After the Justice Department brought its antitrust suit in 1972, the networks divested themselves of much of their production facilities. Now most drama is made by producers and production companies which are independent of the television industry.

Making any kind of film for wide distribution involves a number of large-scale organizations as well as outside financial backing. The systems that have evolved in the United States and elsewhere are similar. Amateur and semiprofessional films can be and are being made by small groups or individuals with relatively little money. However, most of the films shown on prime-time commercial television and in the commercial movie theaters are rarely, if ever, made by a lone entrepreneur with his or her own money. The independent producers of television drama and the large movie studios in the United States must find financial support before a project can be started. Theater movie production usually is supported by banks or through corporate enterprises from which investors buy stock. Each film made represents a gamble on the part of investors who are not guaranteed a profit from their investment. When a film is profitable, the rewards are so great as to make risk-taking worthwhile. The stars, the director, and the script enhance both the chance for financial support and the chances of success.

Movies made for television, the episodic series, and children's animated cartoons are rarely made without support from sources outside the production companies who make the films. An essential difference between a movie made for theater distribution and a television film is that most television dramas receive the outside support from one of the three networks instead of a bank, individual, or corporate structure. Although there are over 20 production companies in Los Angeles making or trying to make television films, only four or five produce most of the drama seen on prime-time television. While the number of networks has remained constant, the number and power of these program suppliers vary from year to year. For example, when I did my study of program suppliers and on-the-line producers who worked for them, the major suppliers were Universal Studios (MCA), Desilu, Quinn-Martin, and one or two others. Now, in 1980, there are several new names among the producers, and a few of the former suppliers are no longer producing for television.[3]

Essentially, there are only three primary buyers for all television drama; the networks. Program suppliers occasionally sell original drama to syndication companies which supply the few independent local stations throughout the country. This practice has increased in the last few years. Norman Lear (T.A.T./Tandem Productions) has done so with some success (*Mary Hartman, Mary Hartman*) and some failure (*All That Glitters*). Also, several stations have formed a cooperative to buy drama directly. However, the program suppliers prefer selling to the networks because the profit is higher and because a successful network show has greater possibility for multiple showings than an originally syndicated show. Most of the successful episodic series (those on the air for two or more seasons) are syndicated for one or more additional

runs. Every program supplier desires to produce a series that is successful enough to be syndicated in the United States through the independent stations and through network television during the daytime or late
evening hours. A very successful series may be shown through syndication by releasing old programs previously on the air during prime time
while still showing new programs of the same series during the evening
hours. Two examples are *M*A*S*H* and *Charlie's Angels*, which were
both seen during the 1979 season on prime time as well as through
syndication at other times of the broadcast day.

The Pilot Film

In former years most of the episodic series that appeared on the air
were presented to the networks for purchase in the form of a pilot film.
The pilot film is still used as a primary source for selection of new
series. However, because the investment in a pilot film is so great, many
are also seen as films which can have wider distribution than simply a
vehicle to show off a program idea. Often a pilot film will also be seen
as a movie made for television. As such it will be shown on the air
several times during a season or repeated in several seasons. In addition,
it will be sold to a syndication company for showings abroad, either in
the theaters or on television (or both). Thus, the investment in the pilot
is profitable to both the program supplier and the network. In addition
to their initial wages, actors, writers, and directors receive residual
payments (royalties) from repeated broadcasts.

Not all pilot films are purchased as series. The networks are involved
in every step of the creative and production processes from story
concept to a successful series. Before a script can be written, the story
idea is presented to one of the network's executives, usually a person in
charge of programming. This is done by conversation, because under
the rules of the Writers' Guild nothing should be presented in writing
without a formal contract. Even after a script is written and purchased
by the networks there is no guarantee that the network will finance the
pilot film. When a script is completed, it is the property of the network.
However, contracts are usually written so that the program supplier is
free to try to sell the script elsewhere should the original contracting
network reject it. If not satisfied with the script, the network has the
option of asking for rewrites either from the original author or from

someone else. If and when the network is satisfied, a contract for a pilot film is negotiated with the program supplier.

The Series

Most pilots do not become episodic series. The network along with the advertisers decide whether or not to place an order with the program supplier for a certain number of additional scripts and films to be produced if they think the pilot will make a successful series. This order may be for as few as four or six but the usual minimum order is 12 or 13 (to be shown for half a season). After a show is on the air for three or four weeks and there is some indication of audience approval, a decision is made whether to order more scripts and films. If ratings are low and advertising support is no longer forthcoming, the series will be cancelled. In reality, this means that no further shows will be ordered. A series which is on the air for 13 weeks or less usually disappears from the air, never to be seen again by any audience.

Many shows that finish a season are renewed for a second season. There are examples of successful series which remain on the air for five, six, seven, or more years. Such shows are very profitable to the networks, program suppliers, the creative people working for the production houses and the local broadcaster. As mentioned earlier, these shows are usually syndicated and often shown repeatedly on independent stations throughout the program day and on the network stations during the late evening and during the day. Also, they are often seen abroad, both in developing and developed nations.

Because of the potential profit associated with the episodic series, their initial costs are very high. According to *Broadcasting* magazine, neither the networks nor the program suppliers are anxious to divulge the specific costs of a prime-time series. Producer Grant Tinker, head of MTM productions, a very successful program supplier who had five series on the air during the 1974-1975 season, contends that because costs are so high producers are underpaid by the networks for first-run dramas. According to Tinker, it is impossible for a show to pay for itself from the original sale (*Broadcasting*, 1974). Most of those I interviewed as far back as 1968 agreed that it is unlikely for a show to recover costs while in its first run (before syndication) even if it were on the air for several years. This means that the real profit from the production of prime-time drama must come from reruns and syndication.

The networks at the present time are dependent on the program suppliers for ideas, scripts, and actual productions. In the late 1960s the suppliers' power was even more pronounced than it is at the present time because each network also operated as a program supplier producing drama directly. *Bonanza*, for instance, was produced by NBC. In 1972 the Justice Department brought antitrust actions against ABC, CBS, and NBC for alleged monopoly practices. Although the suit has not been settled, the result of bringing the action is that the networks produce fewer of their own programs than they did in the recent past. At this writing, the Justice Department has reached an out-of-court settlement with NBC. The agreement imposes a number of restrictions on NBC in the programming area, but those restrictions are not effective unless ABC and CBS agree. Since the Justice Department suit was filed, the Federal Trade Commission (FTC) also began preliminary inquiry into broadcasting antitrust questions. The allegations being considered by the FTC, the Justice Department, and the FCC are that the networks have monopolized and restrained trade in prime-time programming. The Justice Department agreement with NBC will prevent the network from producing any television entertainment programs or feature films, but the network will still control scheduling including choice of programs and time. This agreement does not prevent the networks from financing the productions of pilots; it simply prevents the networks from producing the films directly.

The program production companies hire the creative people, actors, writers, directors, on-the-line producers, and other personnel who actually create the films. Thus, the producers function as the liaison between the networks and the creators of drama. The networks deal with the production companies (program suppliers) for a flat fee plus a share of the syndication rights. The networks claim they are as dependent on the program suppliers as the suppliers are on them. The mutual dependency that has evolved between the networks and program suppliers is clear. In reality, although production companies provide new ideas for the shows and the actual films, the networks decide whether these ideas are accepted. The networks sometimes accept new ideas. Both the content and form of television drama have changed since television first became a national mass medium. However, no matter how creative a program supplier is, most television drama seen each season is the direct result of network policy and decision-making.

NETWORKS, RATINGS,
AND ADVERTISING

Network profits come from advertising revenue. Network advertising rates climbed 30 percent in 1977 and have been going up ever since. In 1973, the advertiser paid $125,000 a minute for a spot on a show rated in the top ten. In order to attract advertisers, the number of viewers becomes the important consideration for program selection. The cost of a commercial spot is calculated to the all-important cost per thousand viewers (CPM). Thus, if a program attracts more viewers than another show, the profit to the network increases.

It is almost impossible for the networks or anyone else to predict with any certainty whether a new dramatic show will attract a large enough audience (measured by the ratings) to be profitable. Decisions on what to show appear to be made on the previous track record of the program supplier, what has been popular during a previous season, and often on "instinct." Although some kinds of audience pretesting surveys are made on certain shows before they are added to the schedule, these measures have proved unreliable (although they are still used). The two ways shows are pretested, either by presenting the plot idea verbally or on paper to a sample of viewers or by pretesting the pilot film with a captive audience, has not guaranteed more successful shows.

Martin Seiden (1974) has suggested that television drama is not under the control of the networks, but rather under the control of the A.C. Nielsen Company, whose rating services are treated as gospel by the networks and advertisers. I agree that after a show is developed and scheduled, the ratings obtained from Nielsen are very important. The networks have the most power in deciding what will be broadcast. They select the shows for their first run on the air. The ratings determine what will stay on the air. An episodic series is considered a success when there are two or more seasons of episodes available for syndication. For a series to stay on the air for more than its initial run, it must secure high ratings. The ratings of a miniseries and a movie made for television are also important to profits. For all kinds of drama, the ratings determine both the cost of the commercials to the advertisers and the profits to the networks and program suppliers.

Ratings—A Definition and Explanation

Ratings are estimates, mostly projections, obtained from sampling techniques. They are expressed most often in the following ways: (1)

the percentage of sets in use or homes watching television in the area being sampled at a given time (ratings), and (2) the percentage of the audience a particular program is drawing in comparison with those programs being televised at the same time (share). Over 200 broadcast-rating services or audience-research firms exist in the United States. The largest and most powerful is the A. C. Nielsen Company.

Advertisers and advertising agencies rely on Nielsen ratings in buying more than $900 million worth of network television time and programs each year. Along with the national television networks, they have invested over $20 million annually in Nielsen contracts. Each of the major networks alone spends over $300,000 for various audience-research reports and relies on Nielsen for 90 percent of their information.

The basic component of the Nielsen broadcast research operation is an automatic recording device called an audimeter. The device is wired, out of sight, to the television set in each of some 1,160 participating sample homes which comprise Nielsen's fixed panel. When the set is in operation, the audimeter records minute-to-minute set tuning on 16mm film in a cartridge that is changed every two weeks by the set owner. From the data gathered from the audimeter cartridge and from diaries, the Nielsen Company computes both local and national data for the television industry and issues information to subscribers through a variety of reports released at various intervals. Of all the reports, the Nielsen Television Index is perhaps the most influential in the industry. It includes (1) estimates of the number of U.S. television households using television at various times (*rating*); (2) average audience (homes viewing during an average minute of a program); (3) total audience (homes viewing the program in excess of five minutes); (4) the *share* of the audience during the average program minute, according to the number of sets actually in use at the time; (5) the average audience by programs' time segments; and (6) the number of stations and programs covered. Also included are sponsor and program indices, audience estimates by sponsorship, program-type audiences, television audience trends, and a national ranking of top programs.

There is little controversy that the Nielsen ratings are a powerful force in American broadcasting. The Nielsen ratings are considered to be official by the advertisers for the national market. Les Brown (1971) asserts that the Nielsen ratings are the real product of American television. They are what the networks sell to the advertisers and what the programs are designed for. For example, if a show has a 20 rating at 8:30 p.m., it supposedly reaches 25 million people. The rating can be broken down to "demographics," that is, the ages, sex composition, regions of the country, and income categories. The advertisers buy numbers and particular demographic subsamples. Brown contends that a sponsor who places his commercial in a time spot may not even know the name of the program he is sponsoring.

The two sets of numbers which are prime indicators of success or failure of a show are the rating and the share. In network television, a national rating of 17 or more is generally satisfactory in prime time. This indicates that 17 percent of American homes are tuned in to the particular program. The share, as noted above, is a competitive evaluation, denoting how a given program is performing opposite others on the air at the same time. A show usually does not survive unless it receives a share of 30.

Before 1970, the commercial value of a network television program was judged simply in terms of the percentage of households and the share a particular programs attracted. Since that time demographics (especially age, income, and sex) of each program's audience has become crucial. According to Barnouw (1978), when the magazine concept of placing commercials was widely adopted, slot-buying became highly scientific. Nielsen data can tell a sponsor the male/female composition of the audience and can break the audience into age groups. In addition, because Nielsen conducts marketing research for products as well as audiences, sponsors can get matching demographic information on their retail customers for any of their products. Thus, sponsorship became a matching exercise—the demographics of the audience against the demographics of the buyers of the products.

Program Survival

Network programs and especially dramatic series tend to survive, not if the content pleases the advertisers or the networks, but on other criteria. One necessary requirement for survival is the size of the audience. The other is if the audience meets the demographic requirements of the sponsors. Many sponsors are mainly trying to reach women, especially those between the ages of 18 and 49, because the products most commonly advertised are drugs, cosmetics, soaps, and other household products. Thus, survival of a program depends on high ratings as well as an audience with the necessary demographic requirements. High ratings alone are not enough to ensure survival. Some contend that the ratings, because they are scientific, are a democratic means of determining audience demand (Seiden, 1974). Others disagree on the basis that certain groups are not included in the consideration of what is meant by demand. It is clear that programs are not designed for everyone, but rather for specific audiences. For the most part, minority audiences and those with less money for consuming, such as intellectuals, and the aged, who in particular make up a large segment of viewers, are rarely considered by the program suppliers and the networks. This will be further discussed in Chapter 6.

THE LOCAL STATIONS

According to the Communications Act of 1934, individual stations, not the networks, are licensed and held accountable for what is broadcast. Many citizen groups and critics have argued that a local station, by affiliating with a network, actually forfeits its local responsibility. They contend that because the networks have complete control over programming (especially prime-time), they are not merely suppliers but virtual dictators.

Although there has always been some concern over the relationship of the networks and the affiliates, this concern increased during the late 1960s and 1970s. Pressure from one chain of local affiliates (Westinghouse) led to the Prime Time Access Rule discussed in Chapter 3 (Howard, 1979). The dissension between networks and affiliates has grown because of a major shift in the economics of television. In 1976, many major companies sharply increased their national budgets for television advertising. This resulted in increased demand for television commercial time, a shortage of commercial time available, and increased rates by the networks for this time. Under agreement with the affiliates, network commercial time is traditionally limited to three minutes per prime-time half hour. A half-hour dramatic show is approximately 20 minutes long. This leaves approximately seven minutes for promotions, station breaks, and commercials to be sold at the local level. This three-minute limitation on the networks only applied to shows made for television. Movies made for theater distribution (and sports events) were exempt from the limit. In 1976 the networks redefined what qualified as a movie to include movies made for television, miniseries, and extra-length versions of regular programs.

According to a study by Howard (1979), during the 1976-1977 television season 25 percent of all prime-time half-hour segments contained three and one-half minutes of network commercials instead of the acceptable three minutes. The result of this increase meant that local stations were denied the time to sell two or more commercials (a commercial spot is usually 30 seconds long).

Affiliates have argued that network control of programming limits diversity as well as their profits. In June 1978, the FCC started the first investigation into network operations since 1955. The final report from the investigation will not be submitted until the middle of 1980. As with all such investigations, no major changes in broadcasting operations are expected.

Nonetheless, most local stations are not necessarily committed to diversity or higher quality programs, but to higher profits, as are the networks. Although the differences among the three networks may be minimal when it comes to overall programming, differences exist in terms of ratings that vary from year to year. For many years, CBS shows received the highest ratings, followed by NBC and ABC. In the last few years ABC's ratings have been the highest. This has changed the network affiliate structure somewhat. During the years 1977 and 1978, one station a month left either CBS or NBC to join ABC. At the same time, affiliates have shown an increased tendency to resist network pressure and look elsewhere for programming. Several years ago, a group of stations joined Tel Rep, a national advertising sales company, to form Operations Prime-Time for the purpose of producing alternatives to network dramatic programming. The first production (miniseries), Taylor Caldwell's *Testimony of Two Men,* was very successful. The stations carrying the program were able to bring enough advertising revenue to pay for the program and still make a larger profit than if they had used a network program. This cooperative, which some are calling a fourth network, includes approximately 65 stations which are network affiliates plus 25 independent stations.

Out of the more than 600 affiliated television stations in the United States, 65 might not be considered a great exodus. Most stations want to retain their affiliation with the networks because network affiliation is virtual assurance of station profit. One reason network programming assures profit is that network owned and operated stations reach at least 25 percent of the television viewers in the United States because these stations are in the major market areas. Networks have a strong audience base even without the affiliate stations.

CONCLUSION

The possible future of network control is uncertain, not only because of some affiliate discontent, but because of the technologies available that could bring greater diversity in programming. However, as of now, the three networks decide on most of the dramatic programs televised in the United States. The history of dramatic production since the invention of the moving picture should alert those who are antinetwork that monopoly over filmmaking has always concerned critics, the courts, and Congress. There seems little reason to suppose that the adoption of greater diversity in dissemination will result in a more open system. This will be discussed in the concluding chapter.

The following chapter will discuss how network control influences the craft aspects of film and tape production. Those who create television drama—the writers, actors, directors, and on-the-line producers—are dependent on both the networks and the production companies in order to work. Problems of control as well as problems of employment and unemployment depend on the organizational and industrial structures that finance and disseminate drama.

NOTES

1. In the United States most television is provided by commercial enterprises. There is an alternative system of broadcasting established by the Public Broadcasting Act of 1967, commonly known as public television and radio. Public television is partially supported by the United States government, partially by contributors at the local level, and partially by grants from foundations and business enterprises at both local and national levels. The public system, although national, does not have the financial resources that are available through the networks and advertisers. The number of public stations are fewer than the number of commercial stations, and the audience is smaller as well (Lyle, 1974).

2. The magazine concept of television advertising is similar to buying ads that are interspersed among stories and articles in a magazine. The system adopted in the United States is different from that adopted in England and other countries, where the broadcaster decides where to place commercials, rather than having the sponsor decide.

3. Every Friday, *Daily Variety Western Edition* reports on the television shows in production in the Los Angeles movie and television studios. If a show is on location but made by an L.A. program supplier, that show also will be listed. Similar but not as detailed information is available in *Weekly Variety* for the New York area.

5

HOW CONTENT IS PRODUCED

Production process of television drama. Power relationships among creative people, actors, writers, directors, and on-the-line producers, and how their work is organized. Whether content reflects the values of those working in Hollywood.

This chapter is about the creative people—the actors, writers, directors, and on-the-line producers—who are directly responsible for the programs seen on the air. The production process of television drama can be analytically divided into two functions, those concerned with profit and business details and those concerned with the craft aspects of production (Moore, 1961). Arthur Stinchcombe (1959) considers the craft production process as an organization of groups of "professionalized" (occupationally skilled) individuals performing roles for which they are trained by education or long apprenticeship; these craft workers are represented by craft-type or white-collar unions open only to those in the occupational groups rather than all employees of the industry. Craft workers especially those associated with the arts, value autonomy. Ideally, the creative people associated with filmmaking would like to control the content of the films they make. Although all four occupational groups (actors, writers, directors, and producers) have formed white-collar unions which bargain collectively for each group, the autonomy usually associated with craft work is lacking. Because of the way work is organized in Hollywood, the dichotomy between the craft aspects and the business aspects is a false one.

For the series in particular, the problems associated with high ratings take precedent over all other considerations. The creative people must satisfy the production companies (the program suppliers), the network which distributes the series, the advertisers, and finally a large segment of the audience to keep their show on the air. This chapter will be divided as follows: First there will be a discussion of how work is organized in film and videotape production. This will be followed by a more specific description of the power relationships among the producers, writers, actors and directors. In the conclusion there will be a short discussion of whether the values of the artists (craft-workers) are reflected in the content.

WORK ORGANIZATION

Most, but not all, production of drama takes place in Hollywood. Some drama is filmed, other is videotaped. In this discussion the word film will be used to denote both methods of production. There are differences in content between the two types, but the work arrangements vary only in minor ways that are not relevant to this discussion. Video production usually involves fewer actors and has become the major method used for producing situation comedies, the most popular series form in recent years. Film is used for westerns and adventure and crime shows. For both types, content is selected similarly and through hierarchical arrangements although somewhat varied in different companies. In the television industry, content selection and creation follows a common pattern

From conception of a story idea to the final print, many individuals play important technical and creative roles in filmmaking for television drama While the networks and program suppliers have authority and actual power over the selection of series, movies and other drama, the on-the-line producers actors, directors, writers, editors (cutters), casting directors and others are responsible for the actual tasks associated with filmmaking. Television drama like its artistically favored first cousin, the theater film, is never the product of the lone artist. Working in concert with more or less harmony, the "crew" makes the film that is shown on the air.

During November 1978, there were 20 production companies making television drama for the three major networks. The productions included series, movies, animated cartoons, and some specials. Work was concentrated in five major companies and several minor ones. The major companies are all organized in a similar bureaucratic fashion: The executive producers have responsibility for several shows. Under the executive producers is the on-the-line producer, who is the liaison for the others responsible for the craft aspects of the film, the studio itself, and the network. The cadre of people hired for a film includes the director. actors, and writers who are under the direct supervision of the one-the-line producer. Also working on the set or behind the cameras are grips electricians camera people, wardrobe people, an assistant director, a script clerk, editors, and casting directors. After the filming, the finishing of the film, including music and laughter dubbing, is done by others outside the studio on a contractual basis. A half-hour series episode takes about five days to film, a one-hour episode eight days, and a full-length movie about 15 to 20 working days, depending on the cast and length. In reality, a half-hour series episode is only 20 minutes in length; an hour show only 40 minutes. The time difference between the length of the drama and the program length is made up by commercials, station breaks, and program promotions. The actual making of a drama will be described through the roles of the creative people.

The production and manufacture of television drama are rooted to the business interests in the United States. Consequently, the content must be produced by people who are either willing to suppress deep-seated dissident values (should they have such values) or by people who are fundamentally in agreement with the system. Work in the industry is scarce; there are far more available workers who have both the desire and the ability to create television drama than there is work for them to do. The production companies and the networks have the power to determine who works. Without work there is no opportunity for creative expression in television, and even if a worker is employed in a creative task most of the important decisions about content are made by others. However, once a show is on the air and if it is successful, the power of the creators—especially the on-the-line producers and the star actors—increases substantially. Also, all creators, because the work is craftlike, nonroutinized, and requires daily decisions about events that are not predictable, have influence over the final product. Regardless of how many episodes of a series are made, each production is a unique event and each script, regardless of the formula for the series as a whole, provides some opportunity for creativity.

ON-THE-LINE PRODUCERS

The working producer of filmed dramatic television has a key role and relative power in the selection of content once a show is bought by a network or a syndication company. Producers are in charge of hiring the cast (except possibly the stars), the directors, and the writers. They serve as coordinators between the networks for which the show is produced and/or the program suppliers. The producer also has the final responsibility for cutting and editing the filmed product. This combination of tasks and associated power is common in the role of television producer, but is not necessarily associated with the title "producer" in other media. The producer has many of the tasks that in the motion picture industry (especially in European productions) are assigned to the film director. When a feature film director for the theater films is hired to do a picture, he is given a story to develop and, along with the film editor, cuts the picture. In television drama (miniseries, regular series, and even movies made for television which are often pilots for series) story development is a major function of the producer. Most on-the-line producers are hyphenates, that is, writer-producers or possibly director-producers. It is often said by people associated with the television and movie industries that the feature film is a director's medium while television is a producer's medium. Three on the major creative parts of television dramatic production—story, casting, and editing—are under the producer's control. Although casting is a joint effort among the director, casting director, and producer, the producer has final authority. The directors shoot the picture and, on the set, they are in control. However, since they are hired by the producer, they turn to the producer when problems arise on the set (Cantor, 1971).

In addition, because the producer's major responsibility is story development, he or she holds a position of power over the script writers. The producer hires the writers to do one or more scripts (if it is a series) and often works with the writers for all kinds of dramatic production, directing the tone and outcome of the script. Many free-lance writers aspire to be on-the-line producers because of the relative power and autonomy vested in that role.

Because the producer is a salaried employee working for a program supplier, he or she does not have complete control and is caught in the middle between those above in the networks and production companies and those to be supervised in the production operation. As a representative of management, the producer must fulfill the goals of the organization. Thus, if the ratings of a show are low, the show will be cancelled. Network profits depend on the ratings. No matter how creative or artistic a show may be from a critical perspective, the final determination of whether a show stays on the air is made by the networks. Thus, a producer must deliver a salable product. A producer of a successful series may be able to generate a large amount of power and possibly can communicate both social and political values which are seemingly incongruent with those held by network executives and program suppliers. Most of the time this is unlikely. Ideally, the producer has responsibility for the creative aspects of the show, but this is always delegated authority. Even if the producer owns, creates, and produces the show, the network retains the right to final approval of scripts casts and other creative and administrative matters. Should a producer fight too often with the network over creative decisions, the producer is replaced. Although the producer is the most powerful of the production team, except for the star actors, his or her power is not absolute. As noted earlier, the pool of writers and others, such as assistant directors, who are qualified to work in the capacity of producer far exceeds the demand. The number of teleplays in production at any one time never exceeds 100 and is often less. That figure includes soap operas, prime-time series, movies made for television, animated cartoons, and miniseries. Producers, along with their partners in the creative process, face sporadic employment. A number of examples could be cited where the series was in production for several years with a number of different on-the-line producers. In some cases the producer became disenchanted with the work, but often the network or program supplier replaced one person with another who would be more compliant. Examples are *Star Trek*, *Mannix*, and *Bonanza*. Thus, the success of the series does not ensure the job of the on-the-line producer.

ACTORS—
CREATIVE POWER AND AUTONOMY

The star actors of a successful series are by far the most powerful of the creative people working in television. When an actor stars in a series and that series is a success, the actor becomes the person to whom everyone else, including the writers, directors, and producers, must cater. The series depends on the actor to remain on the air, and therefore the actor's wishes are considered in all aspects of the production process. However, the above is only true for a successful series and not for drama that is unsuccessful, and this power is not transferable to the next series to which a star might become attached. In contrast to the stars, supporting actors—even those who are regulars in a series—are often the least powerful of all the creative personnel. If an actor becomes troublesome, his or her part can be written out of the series. Often when supporting actors become as popular as the star, a new series is developed for him or her. This is known as the spin-off. A successful series, especially those done on tape and in particular the situation comedies, often develop a following and high ratings because of their stars. Many of these shows either are named after the star or have a name which is associated with the actor in the starring role. Examples are *The Mary Tyler Moore Show, The Bob Newhart Show, Rhoda, Lou Grant,* (both spin-offs from the *The Mary Tyler Moore Show*), and *Marcus Welby, M.D.* None of these shows could have remained on the air without the stars appearing as the leading characters. Because of the large profit associated with a successful series, these actors have been able to generate power as long as the ratings remain high.

Actors (and other artists) have generally been perceived apart from others who earn their living from wages, salaries, commissions, and sales. Historically, it might be legitimate to separate the purveyors of culture from those who deal in producing the material artifacts and substance of a society. However, because of the way much work is organized, this is no longer a legitimate separation (if there ever really was one). The growth of mass media industries also contributed to eliminating this separation. Because many artists and intellectuals work in bureaucratic settings and are dependent upon complex technology, they have problems associated with control and autonomy that other workers do not have. Actors have an additional problem: Not only do they work in a bureaucratic setting doing essentially craft work, but actors are directly espousing values and political positions which may or may not be compatible with their own ideological viewpoints. Actors are unable to select the parts they play unless they are stars. Movie stars sometimes are able to produce their own movies and then select the part. There are examples of television stars who are very powerful for a number of years because the series in which they appear have been successes. However, when these same stars try other roles, they often fail or have trouble finding a suitable series and may join the unemployed. Examples are Richard Chamberlain, who was Dr. Kildare, Vince Edwards who was Ben Casey, and even Mary Tyler Moore, who appeared in several successful series and then failed at her attempt to do a variety show. Mary Tyler Moore, with her husband Grant Tinker, owns a production company. Her star status and entree through her own production facilities did not ensure success. The ratings were poor and her variety show in 1978-1979 did not last the season.

Those actors who are not stars are dependent on others who write the parts, produce the shows, and, more importantly, finance and distribute the production. Once an actor receives a part, it is likely that someone else will determine how the role is to be interpreted as well. More than any other occupation which is publicized as glamorous and creative, acting in the United States provides little freedom or autonomy for those who appear on the screen. Because actors are interpreters rather than manufacturers of symbols, they are dependent upon the enterprises that produce the shows.

Actors also have a serious problem in finding employment. As noted earlier, all of the creative people in television have employment problems, but for no other group is the problem as severe as it is for the actors. The actor "labor force" is small compared with other groups. The U.S. Census reported only 23,430 actors in 1970 (NEA, 1976). Most screen and television actors belong to the Screen Actors Guild, which has 39,000 members (18,000 in Los Angeles). The discrepancy in figures is due to differences in defining an actor (see Cantor and Peters, 1979). Because the Guild has many members who work in other media or other occupations, the figure is clearly inflated. Moreover, the Guild reports that only 15 percent of its members work at any one time. There are only about 2,000 acting jobs available in Hollywood for about 18,000 people, if one takes the Guild figures seriously.

One might ask why the Guild does not limit membership on some criteria. Every actor and union official to whom Anne Peters and I have spoken has been firm about defining an actor. All agree that any actor should have a chance to compete for a part in a production regardless of background or present status. The producer, director, or casting director are the people with the right to decide who gets hired. The only obligation the Screen Actors' Guild has is to provide good working conditions once a member is on the job. When a nonmember is hired for a part, then by the rules of the Guild he can join the union.

An obvious structural feature which contributes to the oversupply of actors is that television work is casual and similar to seasonal work in other industries. Jobs tend to be of an ad hoc and short-term nature, and there is little continuity of employment. Only stars and regular supporting casts of an ongoing television series have work that lasts more than a few weeks. Theater movies, movies made for televison, and other productions such as TV commercials provide work of short duration.

As noted throughout this section, the differences between the stars and nonstars are outstanding. It is beyond the scope of this book to discuss why certain actors become stars and others do not, but the star system, because it exists, is a powerful force in and of itself. All actors have the possibility of becoming stars, and with that status comes great financial and reputational success. Acting is one of the few occupations, along with professional sports and other related artistic endeavors, which provide a vehicle for the attainment of personal success and fame. There is the opportunity for a few to begin with virtually no capital or credentials and become eminently successful as actors. It is this feature of the occupation which probably explains the tenacity of some actors in the face of deprivation and compromise. However, this feature of the occupation also contributes to why the supply of actors remains large while the demand remains low. And that is not the only reason—acting is an attractive occupation and actors love their work. Every actor interviewed would not only like to work regularly if possible (as is to be expected) but also recognize that working under the present conditions would not guarantee them artistic freedom and certainly not political freedom in the marketplace.

WRITERS

Writers, like actors, are usually freelance; that is, a show uses various writers to write each episode. The unemployment problem for writers is similar to that of actors. However, the Writers' Guild has not encouraged a large membership of the unemployed. Rather, that guild has two classes of membership based on earnings through writing. Thus, the Guild acts similarly to other craft and white-collar unions. However, neither the Writers' Guild nor the Screen Actors' Guild helps its members secure employment. Actors and writers are on their own to find work in an industry where work is scarce and where hiring often depends on characteristics, such as beauty and personality for actors and personal connections with important industry people for writers, other than talent, training, or skills.

The relationship of the writers to the producers has been discussed in detail (Cantor, 1971:92-105). I found in my interviewing of writers that they are closest to the stereotype of the lone artist of any of the creative people in Hollywood. Most writers say that they would like to write drama or other fiction which is more highbrow or socially significant than the material they must write for television.

Joan Moore describes the full-time television writer as having little or no control over any aspect of their writing, except the invention of dialogue and incident. "Their work is rewritten as a matter of routine. It may be changed without their consent by a story editor, producer, director or actor" (Moore, n.d.: 92). My work in Hollywood and New York bears out Moore's contention. Producers have to worry about changes from the network, program suppliers, and advertisers, but freelance writers have to be concerned about everyone in the production process continually changing scripts.

The writer is powerless to control any changes and can only fight about credits which translate into money because of residual payments. The producer and writer are most closely related in function and possibly background. The producer is dependent on the writer for scripts, and the writer is dependent on the producer for assignments. Producers can write scripts because most are by profession writers, but there is not time during a season for them to write all 22 or more scripts that may be needed. Therefore, they assign others, usually writers whose work is familar to them, to write stories that often are developed together. Few if any unsolicited scripts received by the production company are ever considered seriously. The mutual dependency of the writer and producer results in some conflicts. These conflicts may occur over screen credits, because, according to the contract between the Writers Guild and the Motion Picture and Television Producers Association, whoever receives screen credit as the writer receives residuals or royalties if and when the episode is shown as a rerun or as part of a syndicated series. Producers are salaried employees and, while they receive large salaries, they do not receive residuals. Writers freelance and receive payment for their scripts plus residuals when they get screen credit. Because the script is bought outright by the program supplier or producer, changes can be made without consulting the writer. All writers know they are at the mercy of the producer when it comes to control over the script. The producer defends his right to change scripts because it is his job to maintain quality control over the production. Quality control does not necessarily refer only to artistic aspects of the film, but also includes making the scripts in line with the general concept. This is particularly important for a series. The series needs a chief writer responsible for continuing the storyline. If a producer changes or rewrites a script so that a certain percentage is changed, he may wish to receive screen credit so that he can receive the residuals. Most producers are writer-producers, and as writers they are members of the Writers' Guild. But to receive credit they must "prove" through arbitration that they indeed wrote enough of the script to add their names to the credits. The Writers' Guild decides whether the changes warrant the change of credits. Sometimes a producer will try to supplant the writer's name with his own in order to claim all of the residuals.

Freelance writers are used primarily for the adventure, western, and crime shows. In reality, there is no such occupation as television writer. Although there are few writers who write only for television, most write plays, novels, short stories, and, if fortunate, theater films. Very little information exists on writers' work. However, being unemployed as a writer is common, and work for the freelance writer is more precarious now than it was in 1968 and before. This is related to the few movies and television films that use freelance writers as compared with 1968. Presently, because the comedy series are so popular with the production companies, writers are salaried employees as they were in the heyday of Hollywood. For shows such as *Mork and Mindy, The Mary Tyler Moore Show,* and others, a team of writers is hired for the series. This, of course, limits the power of the producer but does not generate much more freedom for the writer. In such situations the "committee" becomes powerful. The writers are assured of their screen credits, but their power is limited in the creative process by the whole production.

If the history of Hollywood were written from the perspective of the occupational roles and structures, one would find that there has never been a clear definition of any of the occupations involved with making a movie. For example, actors direct and write films and often produce them as well. Joan Moore (n.d.) makes the point that besides the difficulty of assigning an occupational role to the various people involved in production, work changes as technology and organization of

Hollywood production changes. She goes on to say that one person in a year's work may create a script in which he or she has complete artistic control and one in which the script is rewritten by others and totally reshaped by directors, actors, producers, and editors. The writer and his role partners are subject to control both from the networks and other distributors as well as those attached to the actual production.

Although space here is limited and the complexities of trying to be a creative writer for television cannot be discussed in the detail the topic deserves, the occupational roles provide the ideal example of how bureaucratic organization affects creative work. Those writers who work as freelancers are no more free from the controls than those who are salaried directly by a production company.

DIRECTORS

Of the four occupational roles discussed here, that of director is the least important. Compared with his counterpart in theater film, the television director is weak and powerless. In television production, he or she rarely stays with the production through the editing process. Directors are hired either on a freelance basis or are salaried regular employees, directing the shows on a weekly basis. When the director is hired for an episode, the time limitations often do not allow him the luxury of his contractual right of the first cut (editing). Thus, the freelance director becomes merely a technician, carrying out the mandates of the on-the-line producers. Only those directors who are hired for a season (again, this is likely in the case of situation comedies) share some authority with the on-the-line producer and the stars to determine content.

CONCLUSION: VALUES AND CONTENT

All four occupational groups discussed have commonalities. They are craft workers who are dependent on others to determine the availability and in some respects the content of their work. All have organized into craft unions which vary somewhat in organization. However, these unions negotiate primarily for monetary payments and working conditions once a member is hired for a job. Other craft unions operate more as true guilds, deciding such things as training requirements and regulating qualifications generally. The unions for creative people, though called guilds, are powerless in determining the content of work. Thus, each of the occupational groups discussed in this chapter is relatively powerless and lacks autonomy.

A primary interest in this book is how the organizational structure and the political and social milieus limit or enhance the freedom of those doing creative work. In 1971, I noted there has been little systematic research of those who create dramatic television. At that time many books and articles had been written for both popular consumption and a more scholarly audience as part of the general critique of the commercial television system (see, for instance, Friendly, 1967; Skornia, 1967; and Miller and Rhodes, 1964). The criticism has not abated. Important books which focus on how influential television is in shaping the psyche of viewers and the social world continue to be written (Mankiewicz and Swerdlow, 1978; Goldsen, 1977). One main theme that threads its way through the criticism is that "while television is supposed to be free, it has become the creature, the servant and indeed the prostitute of merchandising" (Lippmann, 1959).

One argument that is repeatedly made is that commercial programming must appeal to mass tastes. In order for a production to stay on the air, it must reach at least 20,000,000 people. Innovation and creativity are not encouraged because the primary function of the medium as seen by the program suppliers and the networks is to sell airtime to advertisers of products and not to educate, change, or enlighten viewers.

Creators of television drama work for large-scale formal organizations. The methods of social control in the Hollywood studios approximate those of other creators who work in bureaucratic settings. Warren Breed's (1955) classic study showed that journalists were controlled by the reward system and the political preferences of their employers. There is a difference in working in a Hollywood studio, because the creative people in drama must bend to the pressures from both the production company and from the networks, leaving the creative people little control. There are individual differences in the way people adapt to these controls, and some creators clearly agree with those in control. The gatekeeper studies of decision-making in news and entertainment provide evidence of the complex relationships that exist between creators and the programs created. In a review of some these studies, Dennis McQuail (1969) notes that the most significant point to emerge from such work is that the orientation of creators who work in bureaucratic settings is shaped by the structure and culture of the organization in which they work. Paul Hirsch (1978a) makes a similar point, suggesting that occupational craft and organizational norms concerning news and story categories explain the variety in story selection more than personal values.

Herbert Gans (1974) has suggested that all creators of art, whether it is high art or popular art, have similar difficulties in their relationships with larger social structures. All creators are communicating to an audience, real or imagined, even those who create alone in a garret, seemingly removed from the mainstream. According to Gans, the stereotype of the lonely high-culture artist who only creates for herself or himself is false. He also contends that the image of the creators of popular arts who suppress their own values to cater to an audience is also false. However, the results of the research I have conducted led to different conclusions. I agree with Gans that all artists are creating for a real or imagined audience. However, the relationship between the values of the creators and the content they create is very complex. From the interviews I have conducted two similarities stand out. The creators of popular drama understand that the kind of content they create depends on the organizational norms and culture, and that content is primarily controlled by others outside the production process. The most succinct example comes from those who produce the animate cartoons for children. They can and do produce all kinds of content from violent shows to high-level artistic and educational offerings (Cantor, 1972, 1974).[1] Also, all creators, regardless of their position in the production organization, value artistic freedom and control.

Most people who create television drama are "in tune" with what is expected—their values are the same as those who control the production processes. They want to create shows which will sell to large audiences. Others see the creative process (especially for television) as one in which there is continuous conflict and struggle for control. Their values are clearly different from those for whom they work. However, those people who have values which cannot be reconciled with the mandates from above are usually forced out of the system. Most people who want to stay in television production usually knuckle under to pressure. Most say that in order to earn a living or to learn their craft, they accept parts or write what is acceptable to the production companies and the television networks. However, their ultimate goal is to be able to create art which is either more aesthetic or more socially and politically relevant (Cantor 1971, 1974). In other words, they are creating for an audience, not necessarily the ultimate viewers, but those who control the production process. If their audience were directly receiving the content, the product might be different. However, the viewers do not see what is produced until several months after it is created. Each script and film has been approved and censored by others who are directly involved in the production process. These others are network officials (especially the network censors), executive producers or production company heads, and others who have approval rights. Thus, script writers and filmmakers are creating for the decision makers primarily and only secondarily for the wider audience which is too large and amorphous to consider seriously.[2]

Up to this point I have used the word "values" rather loosely. A value is a conception of what is believed to be desirable for either the individual or the group. In particular, values relating to the political and the aesthetic are important here. These values the creators hold, may or may not be communicated through television drama. Creators of drama are a heterogeneous group. The value differences among actors (Peters and Cantor, 1978), musicians (Faulkner, 1971), producers, and writers (Cantor, 1971, 1972, 1974) are substantial. However, the orientation of those creators to their work and to the act of creating (judged by what they say and the content they produce) is shaped only partially by their values. As argued throughout, the marketplace, the work organizations, the means of dissemination, and the legal structure all contribute to the kind of content (or art) seen on television.

The aesthetic values of the writers and producers are clearly disparate from those associated with television drama. Nearly all producers and writers I interviewed think most television dramas are aesthetically poor. Many consider themselves more talented or creative than is evident from their television work. The question of political values is more complex. There is no agreement on what political values, if any, are being communicated through television drama (see Chapter 2). Many writers and producers identify themselves as liberal. They define liberal as being pro-racial integration, pro-mental health and in favour of other socially progressive causes. However, almost all are pro-capitalism: Only one producer identified himself as a socialist. The one political value all espoused was that creative freedom or autonomy is a right associated with artistic production. Although this value is not always recognized as political, here it is being identified as such. The reasons should be obvious. In every totalitarian state, the creators of art are repressed and often jailed for artistic expressions considered detrimental to the state. How this commitment to artistic freedom is translated into the drama is open to debate.

Whether or not the liberal orientation of the writers is reflected in drama is also debatable. Ben Stein (1979), who worked for both Richard Nixon when he was president and Norman Lear (Lear is considered one of the most liberal television producers), thinks television dramatic production, because it is based almost totally in Los Angeles, reflects Hollywood "life styles" more than personal deep-seated liberal philosophy. Stein, who is defined as a conservative, acknowledges that most writers and producers are social liberals, but he contends that the liberalism only goes so far. The actual debate is not over how liberal the writers and producers are, but rather if their values are reflected in the programs. Michael Robinson (1979) suggests that the liberal values of the writers and producers are more evident in present television dramatic content than they were ten years ago. Todd Gitlin (1979), writing from a Marxist perspective, agrees. Gitlin sees these changes as simply cosmetic, noting that the content supports the status quo rather than portraying genuine revolutionary change.

The producers and writers believe they are providing entertainment which by definition, according to them, is apolitical. For example, the producers see the pressure group activities in the 1970s as repressive (*TV Guide*, 1977) because the pressure groups are infringing on their artistic freedom. Many of these producers have some power to fight repression as they define it. The Family Viewing Hour controversy detailed in Chapter 3 is a case in point. Here the program suppliers, the guilds, and others joined to fight for what they perceived as their right to artistic control. However, the power of these producers over the other creative people working on the films is clear. On-the-line producers and star actors have some power to fight for their ideas, but most of those in the ranks must suppress controversial political and artistic values in order to work in the television industry. The way films for television are made ensures bureaucratic control and necessitates organizational compliance from those working as writers, directors, and actors.

NOTES

1. The same people who make Saturday morning shows also produce the animated portions of *Sesame Street*. Production companies, discussed in my earlier work (Cantor, 1972, 1974), who make children's shows have a variety of films in production, ranging from educational ones for the schools (such as depicting polar coordinates on a graph) to artistic animations of classical stories.

2. Creating for television is a social activity, as is the work of all creators (see Tuchman, 1978) and as such can be studied differently from the way I have done here. This is a structural analysis to show how outside and inside organizational constraints limit professional autonomy which writers and producers claim to value highly.

6

AUDIENCE CONTROL

Perspectives on how the audience influences the content of television drama. Some people believe the audience is very powerful (demand perspective). Some believe the audience is powerless (Marxists, neo-Marxists and mass society theorists). Some believe the audience is moderately influencial (social scientists).

Whereas it is relatively simple to describe the nature of production, it is quite problematic to discuss the relationship of the audience to the production process. Not only do scholars and critics disagree on the nature of the audience, they also disagree fundamentally on the impact of the audience on the content. These disagreements are essentially the same as those critics and theorists have concerning the nature of society and human behavior. In this chapter, the discussion will be somewhat different from the preceding chapters. The question being posed is: How does the audience influence content? Because the answer to the question is problematic, several important but varying perspectives on how the audience has been conceptualized will be presented. It will be shown that these varying perspectives are fundamental to how people view the audience's power in the production process. As one might surmise, some people believe the audience is very powerful, some think the audience is only moderately powerful, and some believe the audience is powerless. In addition, within each perspective there are variations and conflicts.

The first part of the chapter will be devoted to what is being termed here the "demand" model. Adherents of this perspective believe that the market determines content. Most broadcasters, some producers, and others (such as market researchers) consider the audience very influential in determining content—in fact, the most powerful influence on content. In contrast, social scientists and other scholars are less convinced about the audience's power to determine content. At one extreme are the mass society theorists and some Marxist scholars who believe that the audience is helpless. Although these theorists may vary when explaining the audience's lack of power, both mass society theorists and Marxists agree that demand is created by those who control the marketplace. The similarities and differences between the two approaches will be discussed in the second section of this chapter.

Mass society theorists generally believe the audience is helpless and that technology and industrialization are responsible for popular culture. Marxists and neo-Marxists, although differing in several respects, have at least one commonality: they both believe that content is the result of the capitalist system. Proletariats (workers) are usually seen as passive recipients of the content, and those who control the means of production and dissemination are either consciously or unconsciously using popular culture, such as drama, as a means of social control to maintain the status quo.

In the third section of this chapter those who hold a middle position about the influence of the audience will be discussed. Most people who present either a functional or systems analysis see the audience as having an indirect but active input into the creation of content. This section is labeled the sociological approach.

The material available on the audience is vast. However, most studies of the audience address questions relating to the effects of the content on viewers, the uses and gratification the content has for viewers, or descriptions of the audience. Essentially, this chapter focuses on what impact the audience has on the communicators, defined as both decision-makers (such as network officials), producers and advertisers, and creators (such as writers, actors, and directors). Because there are almost no studies addressing this question that specifically relate to television drama, the discussion often will go beyond prime-time drama and consider television, popular culture, and mass media generally. Whenever possible, however, the problems relating to the creation of television drama in particular will be examined. The study of mass media has been separated by some from the study of popular culture. Because prime-time drama is one kind of content that can be defined as both television content and a popular art form, I will draw from both traditions where relevant.

Content is produced by people who work in organizations and who are limited or enhanced by government and industrial policies. To study the impact of television it is necessary to know how the content gets on the air and how the content changes (Comstrock et al., 1978; Gans, 1974). Yet, most investigators, even those who advocate studying creators and the decision-making process, find it difficult to include the audience as one element of the total system. Based on a realistic assessment of the production process, the political milieu in which television is programmed, and the size of the viewing audience for successful shows, it is difficult to decide how to measure "feedback" from the audience. Not only is the audience very large for most dramatic programs (anywhere from 20,000,000 to 50,000,000 or more), but the production of television drama takes place months before it is viewed nationally. Under these circumstances it is difficult to conceive of how the audience might have direct input into the creative process. Textbooks on communications present models of how the communication process takes place. The most simple formulation is one in which the communication information flows in a reciprocal fashion from the initiating source to the receiver, who in turn becomes an initiator who sends feedback in some fashion to the communicator (see Schramm, 1973). This model clearly works for face-to-face communicators, but must be modified to be applicable for television viewers. There is little opportunity for those in front of the television sets to send simultaneous feedback to the source.[1]

The way the production of drama has been organized since the early nineteenth century has made simultaneous feedback difficult even when the audience is viewing a live theater production. Writers create plays which are financed by entrepreneurs. Plays are presented after many rehearsals. A theater play, because of its costs, must be written and produced long before an audience sits in a theater. There is some direct feedback at tryouts before the main run of a play, but changes at that time can be only minor. Plays either succeed or fail after they are created. Most drama produced in industrial societies is written by those who hope the critics and paying audience will like it. Although drama critics have exceptional power in live theater, they, along with the paying audience, can only veto or vote for a production. With the advent of the film, even the tryout is almost impossible. Thus, for the film shown in the theater there is even less opportunity for direct feedback than there is for a live dramatic production. Hollywood films are often premiered before they are widely distributed to the general public. Occasionally two different endings will be tried out before audiences to see which one has the most appeal.[2] However, generally it is the box office where the public decides whether a film is a success or failure. Again, the audience only has veto power. For television drama, even those filmed or taped before a live audience, there are few second chances for changes in script or ideas. A pilot film storyline can be changed before it becomes an episodic series. However, because films are produced months before they are shown on the air, the only power the audience has is to turn off the sets.

THE DEMAND MODEL

Given that broadcasters and advertisers understand the reality that direct feedback is almost impossible, the question might be asked: Why do some believe the audience is the main directing force responsible for the content of drama? The answer to that question is very simple, and can be considered a tautology.

Because television is a marketing medium, it must present programs which appeal to a large number of viewers. The argument is made that television drama represents the desires of the viewers. This is justified by reiterating what the networks, the rating services, and the local broadcasters insist is true: Ratings are indices of audiences' wishes. This view of the audience is not necessarily one in which the audience is active and seeks entertainment with certain content; rather, the audience is simply a market for products. Content is seen as "mere entertainment" which is presented by an industry that is competitive, an open marketplace where those who sell the most receive the greatest rewards. What television is selling is not the drama, but the audience. The market system is made up of those who are in staff positions and make decisions about how to appeal to viewers and those on the line who are making the drama. Decisions on what to produce are based on the sales of the previous season, on the results from marketing research, and often on intuition. In the case of television drama, those making the decisions are the network officials. Those on the line try to please the networks by making shows which will attract the most viewers with the right demographic characteristics. Behind all of this is the sponsor who will keep the drama on the air if and only if the drama reaches those people who are potential buyers of the products the sponsors manufacture. The audience in this formulation is not necessarily a mass (large, heterogeneous, and anonymous to the decision makers), but rather a buying public, consumers of a certain age, sex, and income.

Martin Seiden (1974:156) contends that ratings determine content because the structure of the television industry is such that maximum rewards are obtained when the largest numbers of people with the right demographic characteristics are tuned in. The ratings from this perspective are compared with votes. The system is defended by network officials and those who obtain the ratings as being democratic. A.C. Nielsen, for instance, has said,

> After all, what is a rating? In the final analysis it is simply a counting of the votes ... a system of determining the types of programs that the people prefer to watch or hear. Those who attack this concept of counting the votes—or the decisions made in response to the voting results are saying in effect: "Never mind what the people want. Give them something else" [quoted in Sandman et al., 1972:208].

This formulation of the audience as the most powerful influence on dramatic content is relatively simplistic. Although most investigators agree that the process being described does approximate reality, most also believe that by simply saying the audience gets what it desires leaves many questions unanswered. How does content change? How do creators know what will be popular with the audience since there is so little feedback? Why have some programs which have had a relatively small audience when first broadcast been able to build audience interest? In addition, the demand formulation treats television drama only as a business. Several producers I interviewed suggested that television dramatic production could be compared with the manufacture of automobiles. Producers, network officials, and others involved in the selection and creation operate as intrepreneurs who are dependent on consumers to approve of their product. The fact that the product they are creating is an art form is simply ignored. Under the demand formulation, the content comes from the creators who, through knowledge gained either from mystical intuition or through rational processes (such as marketing research), are simply conduits for their audiences.

Most serious analysts of culture industries are aware that the number of available goods (drama, in this case) can exceed the number that can be successfully marketed (Hirsch, 1972). Subsequent to their production, dramas are processed by a selection system described previously.

The actual filtering takes place in the production companies and through the networks. Neither of these organizations is able to decide with any certainty whether a drama will succeed with the "voting" public. However, a reality of this screening and selection is that producers and network officials make decisions with the ratings in mind. The perceived likes and dislikes of some audiences operate as one basis of selection. This notion of the audience being in the heads of the creators and disseminators will be brought up again when I discuss the sociological approach to the role of the audience in the production process. In the examination of factual material about selection and creation of drama, it is obvious that other factors beyond ratings must be considered. The creators and selectors of drama often do not know what the audience might desire. That is clear after examining the number of shows which fail each season (for example, see *Newsweek*, 1979). Also there is no way to know if shows which were passed over might have been very popular.

Nonetheless, the demand model has provided the rationale for the system as it now exists. Those who fail to capture the right audience do not remain in their respective positions, and those whose shows get high ratings are very successful.[3] Writers, actors, and producers must reach the target audience to remain in production. Network officials are fired when the shows they pick are not attractive to the right audience. Thus, the selection and creation of drama within the framework of an industrial model attribute great power to the consumer.

The system as it exists may be the most efficient for reaching the audience desired, but it allows little direct input from the audience into the creative process. Critics are not defined as part of the audience. Citizen groups are seen as pressure groups who hold minority viewpoints; they are rarely considered the target audience. Although citizen and other pressure groups are sometimes placated when they become very vocal, network officials and producers define them as different from viewers. Because critics and protesters are perceived as a minority, those who produce and select content consider their protests as both limiting free speech and as anitdemocratic (*TV Guide*, 1977).

The demand model has been criticized from many perspectives. The conservative critics suggest that defining the audience as those who will buy the advertisers' products limits the creativity of the creators. Moreover, television drama is seen simply as the tool of merchandisers. Most of these critics believe that all popular culture, and television drama in particular, has negative effects on the viewers. The audience, under this formulation, may like the programs, but television brainwashes and controls. This brainwashing is either in the form of alienating psychological effects (Goldsen, 1977) or false consciousness or both. Radical critics also see the content as destructive; it is a means of social control whereby the ideology of the capitalist class is communicated to maintain the status quo, to stifle criticism of capitalism, and to generate complacency in the working classes. The conservative criticism grew out of mass society theory, and the radical criticism can be considered Marxist or neo-Marxist. There are other critics of the demand formulation as well, including the social scientists, educators, and pressure groups who see the system as pluralistic and believe the content of television drama is a public issue. Essentially, they consider themselves part of the audience which is denied access (see Chapter 3 for a fuller discussion).

THE POWERLESS AUDIENCE

Mass Society Theory

The most frequent criticism of television entertainment comes from those who are usually called mass society theorists. This criticism has existed in some form from the onset of industrialization and has been applied to all popular cultural forms. From the inception of the penny press in the nineteenth century there has been great interest in the relationship of the creators of popular art forms and their audiences. One version of the critique of this relationship has its origins in nineteenth-century mass society theory. Mass society theory is far more complex than is being presented here, and there are variations and several modern revisions. One of the most persistent elements in mass society theory has been concern with perceived undesirable, pathological, and threatening changes associated with industrialization and the uses of technology. Mass society theorists have argued that urbanization, industrialization, and the accompanying rise of mass communications have caused traditional communities to decline in importance. Rather than the individual being tied to the family, the church, and the community, he or she is isolated, alienated, and lacking central, unifying beliefs (Kornhauser, 1959:33; Bell, 1961:75). Mass society theorists generally believe that cultural disintegration accompanies social and political disorientation. According to Bell (1961:75), the cultural values and standards of the elite no longer control the mores and values of the mass, and thus these values are in constant flux. Important social thinkers of the nineteenth and early twentieth centuries, such as Henry Maine, Auguste Comte, Herbert Spencer, Max Weber, and Emile Durkheim (see DeFleur and Ball-Rokeach, 1975:133-161), have addressed the transition from a traditional, familial society to a rationalized, industrial society. Industrial societies are characterized as complex, heterogeneous, and differentiated compared with traditional societies which are simple, homogeneous, and undifferentiated (see Bramson, 1961:31). In societies where there is increased occupational specialization (differentiation) and where the population is heterogeneous, adequate linkages between individuals and the growing centralized state do not exist. The social structure disintegrates into two components, the elite, a "qualified," creative, and selective minority; and the mass, an essentially "unqualified," unintelligent, crude mob. This mass may be literate but, because of its lack of classical education, has tastes which are low-level and unselective. In the place of high culture there develops a mass culture which destroys or displaces both high culture and the folk culture of traditional societies. This mass culture "levels the taste of the people, encourages mediocrity, conformity, passivity and escapism" (Gans, 1974:19-64).

Bell and Bramson find that mass society theory springs from the romantic idealism of nineteenth-century Europe, and much of the theory is characterized by emotional attacks on the evils of modern society. Although the theory (or theories of mass society) has been criticized extensively (Gans, 1974; Swingewood, 1977), its influence on how the audience for television is conceptualized has been substantial and, in fact, accounts for the name "mass media of communication" associated with modern, technological means of disseminating information and entertainment.

Mass society theorists have been particularly influential in the way intellectuals have reacted to popular culture and to the popular art forms disseminated by modern technology. According to intellectual critics, mass culture is considered undesirable, in that, unlike high culture, it is mass produced by profit-minded entrepreneurs solely for the gratification of the paying audience. Mass society critics contend that for a cultural industry to be profitable, it must create a low-level, sensational, standardized product. This criticism has been applied to the dime novel, to the movies, to radio, comic books, and to popular music recordings and television drama. The argument states that the commercial system, because it must appeal to mass tastes, limits the freedom of the creators to innovate and express themselves; in addition, the commercial system attracts persons of questionable skills and integrity who use the medium for personal gain at the expense of a public (mass) which is inert and nonactive. This viewpoint is elitist. Although it might be interpreted anticapitalist, it is not. Nineteenth-century critics thought the solution to the problems generated by mass culture was a return to old forms of social relationships, a clear status system with social groups in their respective places. In the period since World War II, the critics have been advocating the elimination of television or possibly more government control. One thing they have in common with earlier critics is that they believe a cultural elite should decide what the audience should see.

Twentieth-century critics generally see the audience as a mass of individuals whose lives are meaningless, empty, and passionless (Ellul, 1964: 378). For instance, Bernard Rosenberg (1957: 7-8) writes:

> Contemporary man commonly finds his life has been emptied of meaning, that it has been trivialized. He is alienated from his past, from his work, from his community. . . . It is widely assumed that the anxiety generated by modern civilization can be allayed, as nerves are narcotized by historical novels, radio or television programs and all the other ooze of our mass media.

According to Rosenberg, neither democracy nor capitalism is responsible for this condition; rather, it is technology. He says, "If one can hazard a single positive formulation, it would be that modern technology is the necessary and sufficient cause of mass culture." The argument has been continued by recent critics of television. For example, Winn (1977), in her criticism of television in the United States, says that there are many aspects of modern life beyond our control. Because people feel increasingly helpless, they depend on television as a substitute for real experience. In turn, television is destructive because the ideas, images, and symbols transmitted through the television screen govern the audience (Goldsen, 1977; Mander, 1978). Television, by the simple process of removing images from immediate experience and passing them through a machine, causes human beings to lose one of the attributes that differentiate them from objects. Jerry Mander (1978), drawing from Jacque Ellul's arguments against technology, asserts that once rid of television, our information field would instantly widen to include aspects of life which have been discarded and forgotten. Human beings would revitalize facets of experience that they have permitted to lie dormant.

> Overall, chances are excellent that human beings, once outside the cloud of television images, would be happier than they have been of late, once again living in a reality which is less artificial, less *imposed*, and more responsive to personal action [Mander, 1978; emphasis added].

Marxist Perspectives

There is not one sociology of art and communications from the Marxist position, but several. Those I have called the mass society theorists perceive weak community ties, technology, and too much leisure for the masses as a threat to culture, art, and true human experience. Unlike this cultural critique of modern industrial capitalism, the Marxists are more concerned with the fate of the potentially revolutionary working class (the proletariat) which, according to Marxist theory, should be ripe for a socialist revolution. The communication media propogate ideology which represents the interests of the capitalist, inhibiting the development of class consciousness. According to Alan Swingewood (1977), "Ideology becomes of crucial importance for the values associated with mass production and consumption of comics, pulp fiction and newspaper combine with the effects of television, cinema and radio to corrupt the proletariat."

When discussing Marxist thought about the production of mass culture and the audience, two separate but related schools of thought are usually compared: The Frankfurt school and the new left critique prevalent throughout the 1970s. The Frankfurt school developed in Germany before the rise of Hitler. Theorists such as Theodor W. Adorno, Max Horkheimer, and Herbert Marcuse, who were trying to explain how fascism was able to flourish in Germany, examined the role of media and popular culture in society. Swingewood distinguishes the Frankfurt group from other contemporary Marxists, because he thinks that the former have lost confidence in the revolutionary role of the industrial working class. For Adorno and Horkheimer in particular, the central fact of capitalist civilization was the progressive collapse of the family as an adequate socializing agent and its mediating function has been passed on to the culture industries. The audience, according to this view, becomes one-dimensional and passive (Marcuse, 1964). The Frankfurt critics are similar to the mass society critics in several respects, especially in the way they both see the media operating to fill a vacuum caused by the way work is organized in capitalist societies. Both schools of thought assert that happiness is identified with material possessions and with the psychological and social integration of the individual into the social order (Swingewood, 1977:12). The difference between the Frankfurt school and variations of mass society theory is in how each views the responsibility for the content. For example, in the *Dialectic of Enlightenment* Horkheimer and Adorno (1973) argue that

> art renounces its own autonomy and proudly takes its place among consumption goods—marketable and interchangeable like an industrial product—aesthetic barbarity become the essence of modern capitalist art, demanding from its subjects "obediance" to the social hierarchy.

Under such a formulation both the creators and the audience have few degrees of freedom. Both are subjects of the system.

The question of why the working class is not revolutionary forms the bases for all Marxist formulations on the media. Basic to the Marxist sociology of art and literature is that all knowledge and art, including mass media content, are formed in the superstructure of society and that the superstructure is conditioned by the mode of production (the economic and material base). The quote from Marx that most often provides the basic rationale for all Marxists analyses on art and media is: "The mode of production of material life conditions the social, political and intellectual life processes in general. It is not the consciousness of men that determines their being, but on the contrary their being determines their consciousness" (Marx and Engels, 1962:363). One's class perspective conditions one's individual perspective. Patricia Clarke (1978), who has summarized the Marxist position on the role of art and knowledge, contends that Marx probed into the roles played by certain ideas in terms of their utility to a certain segment of society.

Marxists and neo-Marxists criticize the content of television as basically supporting the status quo. Although these critics recognize changes in drama since 1950, they agree that the basic messages and values presented on television support the capitalist system. The content is produced either deliberately or unconsciously by those who share the ideology of those who control the means of production and dissemination. The key element is that those in direct control of the drama are also in direct control of the ideas, values, and images that appear on the screen. Thus, in capitalist societies the content of drama reflects the ideology of the capitalists, and the audience is conceptualized as powerless in the selection process of the content to be created. Many who hold this view believe that conducting audience research is irrelevant; and to understand the relationship of the audience to the content, the unit of analysis should be the industrial structures responsible for the content (Janus, 1977; Tuchman, 1974).

However, the problem for present-day critics has changed slightly from the original question raised by Marx and Engels mentioned earlier. Rather than asking why the working class has not revolted, those concerned with American television try to explain the change in content. Several have revised Antonio Gramscie's (1971) concept of hegemony. This concept incorporates the Marxist position on the relationship of the audience to content and goes beyond it. Ideological hegemony refers to an order in which a certain way of life and thought is dominant and to the ways conceptions of reality diffuse throughout all of society's institutional and private manifestations. Hegemony is established by the dominant class (capitalists) who control the means of production and dissemination and becomes so diffused and accepted that it is equated with common-sense knowledge. Hegemony is established to the extent the world view of the rulers is also the world view of the ruled.

The difference between the positions of Gramscie and Marx is somewhat subtle. Marx and those following the classic Marxist position either imply or overtly state that ideology is imposed on the working class by overt control. Gramscie's concept of ideological hegemony suggests that ideology is a shared view and thereby makes direct controls unnecessary. Both the ruling class and the ruled perceive ruling-class ideology as simply "social values" and as the natural state of existence. Raymond Williams (1977), Todd Gitlin (1979), and others address the question: If ideology is imposed as some Marxists contend, why is television drama (and other popular culture) accepted with such enthusiasm by the audience? Although they note the ambiguities in Gramscie, these researchers consider the idea of hegemony a great advance in radical thought because it calls attention to the routine structures of everyday thought, down to common sense itself. This everyday thought works to sustain class domination and tyranny (Gitlin, 1979:252; also see Andrews, 1978).

Gitlin notes that the discussion on hegemony in the literature has been abstract. Rightly, he says that hegemony becomes the answer to all questions concerning the role of ideas and change. Observing that television dramatic content has changed while the interests of the dominant class have not, Gitlin tries to explain the change from the radical perspective and addresses the same questions raised in this chapter. He says that commercial culture packages and focuses ideology that is constantly arising both from social elites and from active social groups and movements throughout the society, as well as within media organizations and practices. Thus, he advocates an approach to studying the media and television drama similar to the one being presented here. He suggests, as do Sallach (1974) and Tuchman (1974), that ideological processes (hegemony) should be studied by looking both to the elites and to the audience.

According to Gitlin, bourgeois ideology is not uniform and there are some conflicts within the elite class. However, the ideological core remains essentially unchallenged and unchanged in television. The commercial system is such that it can absorb and domesticate conflicting definitions of reality and demands. Gitlin does not see the audience as entirely passive. However, when changes in content do come about through pressure of social groups or through other kinds of demands, these changes are cosmetic rather than basic. The basic message of prime-time television, and especially the episodic series, continues to reaffirm bourgeois liberalism because of the focus on individualism and individual solutions to social problems.

The new criticism is somewhat different from the criticism of the Frankfurt school. The Frankfurt criticism was very close to mass society theory suggesting a passive and manipulated audience. The audience is "one dimensional" and the presentation of fantasy through a mechanical device provides the mechanisms for escape rather than action from the masses. In both mass society theory and the Frankfurt school, the audience is unimportant and simply innoculated with the content. The new left critics, possibly because of their own activism, suggest a more active role for the audience. Capitalists are motivated to maintain the audience as consumers must recognize changes in the economic and material roles of the audience. Rather than negating the notion of demand, the radical view extends and reformulates it. It argues that content changes to reflect changes in social and material relations, but not in ways that would encourage revolutionary change. Rather, the content adapts in ways which continue to encourage consumerism to maintain capitalist control. Several of the new left critics explain this adaptation by showing how responsive corporate interests are to changes in consumer ideology. For example, Norene Janus (1977), in her criticism of traditional methodologies that have been used for studying both content and control, notes that the images of women on television have changed in the 1970s. She explains why this change has occurred:

> There have been major changes in the lives of women at both the level of production and ideology and that the material basis for women's oppression is rapidly shifting from the family to wage labor. At the ideological level, women have developed a sense of their own oppression and increasingly resist performing the traditional roles. Corporations, no longer able to ignore these changes in women's lives, have adapted their policies to changing times; the drive for profit has taken a different form in many cases.

In her analysis, Janus sees the profit motive as the single determinant of content. Thus, to sell to women, corporate interests must respond to changes in women's position in society. This formulation differs from the demand model presented earlier in the chapter in one important respect: Women viewers are not getting the content they necessarily want, but the content is determined by others who try to keep women as consumers.

THE SOCIOLOGICAL PERSPECTIVE

Although few social scientists have considered the relationship of the audience to the content, those who have usually approach the subject from a social organizational perspective. Many researchers assume that the nature and significance of communications and popular art forms are determined in large part by the expectations of the communicators and the audience, which tend to be reciprocally related. Others consider economic forces and organizational strategies and present models where the audience and creators are part of the same system (see DiMaggio, 1977; Hirsch, 1978a; Lewis, 1978, for a review). In both cases the creators and audience are examined within an industry or for a particular kind of communication or art form. These analysts criticize both the radical approach and the mass society approach because they believe the core characteristics of any art form can be seen as attributes of the way the art is created, distributed, and marketed (see Gans, 1974; DiMaggio, 1977; Peterson, 1976). Although social scientists see similarities among the various forms of popular arts, they are essentially looking for differences.

Basic to the social organization perspective is the assumption that all creators are communicating to some audience. It is suggested that "writers, broadcasters and political speakers all select what they are going to say in terms of their *beliefs* about the audience" (Riley and Riley, 1959, emphasis added). Ithiel de Sola Pool and Irwin Shulman (1964) claim that the "audience, or at least those audiences about whom the communicator thinks, play more than a passive role in communications." Raymond Bauer (1958) goes one step further, claiming that the audience has much more control over what is communicated, since it is the audience that selects what to read, listen to, or watch. Essentially, Bauer views communication as a transactional process in which both the audience and communicator take important initiatives. Herbert Gans (1957) also has argued that there is active, although indirect, interaction between the audience and the creator and that both effect the final product. Both Gans and Bauer have claimed that their "general feedback hypothesis" is quite different from the theoretical approach that sees the audience as passively receiving what the communicators provide. One problem with this view of the interaction between communicators and audience is that it is difficult to test. It is not known whether feedback as defined by Gans and the Rileys has any effect at all on communicators. They define feedback as information about the outcome of previous messages which changes the definition somewhat from the one presented earlier. Using their definition, feedback does exist as already explained. The ratings and other kinds of audience surveys provide measures for audience preferences and the number of people viewing shows. Both Gans and the Rileys agree that this kind of feedback is indirect, but seem to disagree on whether it is active, as Gans believes, or "obscure and scant" as the Rileys suggest. However, all agree that the impact of information about audience preferences and viewing on the communicator rarely has been scrutinized systematically. Although they wrote over a decade ago, the above statement is still true.

Some explain the content as representing the demands of the audience; others apply a more sociological feedback hypothesis. The differences between these two approaches are qualitatively different. In the *Hollywood TV Producer* (Cantor, 1971), I have taken the position that writers and producers are creating for an audience, but that audience is not necessarily the ultimate audience. Rather, the shows are created for an audience composed of network officials, producers, other gate-keepers, as well as for the writers and producers themselves. Thus, those who write stories and produce the films primarily consider what the buyers and distributers want. This means, of course, that they are very much influenced by ratings and the demographics when they create television drama. Because network officials and others conceptualize their audiences primarily by age, sex, and income, so do the writers and producers. If the target audience was people with certain political or religious beliefs, the content of drama might be quite different. Under this formulation, changes in content come when advertisers and other financial supporters of drama want to reach different target audiences. Joseph Turow (1978) has suggested that when communicators think of their audiences they do so in terms of the rewards they might receive. They construct an audience in their heads which reflects organizational necessities. This description of the relationship of the audience and the communicator is similar to the one I presented in my study of pro-ducers. To work in television, writers and producers, unless very well known or successful, must conform to the norms and policies of the industry. Those writers, producers, and other creators acknowledge the conflicts that arise because they know the audience they must ulti-mately please may be different from the audience they would like to please.

Herbert Gans (1974) and I agree that creators of popular arts would like to impose their tastes and values on the audience. Gans conducted interviews with writers of popular television drama and found that the writers asserted they were always trying to insert their own values into their writing, particularly to make a moral or didactic point. If and when producers objected, the end result was a compromise. Anne Peters and I found the same was true for the on-the-line producers and those actors with some power in the production process. Gans argues, and I agree, that the one major reason for the conflicts that arise between creators and decision makers is because of the class and educational differences between popular culture creators and their audiences.

This conflict manifests itself in several ways: writers conflict with producers and the producers conflict with the production company and the networks over immediate content decisions for a particular show; and some writers, actors, and on-the-line producers have a more basic conflict with the networks concerning who should be the audience. In the first instance minor disagreements over content end in compromise, and major disagreements end with the writer or producer being forced out of the industry. The second kind of conflict is more fundamental but less influential. Several producers and actors have suggested that the networks are losing a potential audience because television drama is too simplistic. If the goal were to reach a different segment of the audience, television series and other drama as well would be different. However, they know that they do not have the power to redefine the audience.

All of the above provides a justification for understanding the system of how drama is created. Rather than simply discussing television or popular culture, system analysis or organizational set analysis has the advantage of discussing each culture industry. Those studies of other cultural production point out common areas in creating popular art forms, as well as the differences between various kinds of culture. The creation of popular drama is similar to the creation of phonograph records, novels, and theater movies: All are high-risk businesses. On the one hand there is a demand for new and possibly innovative drama each season, and on the other hand there is difficulty having new ideas accepted by decision makers. The networks and the sponsors are unable to predict with certainty what the audience will prefer each season. Most decisions seems to rest on a combination of the previous record of success of the production company and the actors involved when selecting a new show. The critics, pressure groups, and others, along with the target audience (the market), are considered as well. Two questions are usually asked: What would a certain group (or groups) do if a program is aired? Will the target audience watch the show? Thus, programs are selected not only to please the target audience, but also to avoid offending powerful pressure groups.

Throughout this chapter the use of the term "audience" has been abstract. The ultimate audience is composed of those people who watch television drama. However, there are other audiences as well. Critics and pressure groups, network officials, advertisers, and others are important audiences. Thus, the audience for each program on the air may be different from the audience in the heads of the creators. Both radical critics and those who take a social organizational approach to studying the mass communication process and the creation of content have suggested that to understand the influence of the audience on content more complex and different approaches are necessary. To understand the role of the audience, several radical critics have suggested the audience should be studied through ethnography and phenomenology (Gitlin 1979; Sallach 1974). Charles R. Wright (1975), who is often cited as presenting the dominant paradigm, makes a similar suggestion. He asks: What are the folkways, mores, and laws that determine who should be members of a particular audience? How should they behave while playing the role of audience, and what are their rights and obligations in relation to others in the audience, to the performers, and to members of the society not in the audience?

CONCLUSION

In the Chapter 5 the question was raised of whether creators were expressing their own values or those of the organizations which hire them. In this chapter the question is raised of whether creators and decision makers are expressing their own values or those of their audiences. It has been argued that producers, writers, and perhaps actors as well are of a different social class from the target audience for television drama. Not only are their values different, but they are better educated, possibly more liberal, and claim to be more "high brow" than the viewers of television drama (Cantor, 1971:164-187).

The creators have few degrees of freedom if they wish to stay in the business; and the ultimate audience, too, is limited to what is presented, simply having veto power. Also, certain publics are clearly being denied programs they might want to view through commercial television. Martin Mayer (1979) has argued that television drama in the '70's was the result of how the audience is defined. Moreover, he suggests that if pay television which mostly presents movies and drama, eventually is utilized by one-half the audience, those who do not subscribe will be offered limited dramatic fare. Although the demand formulation only answers part of the question about control of prime-time television, it does provide one justification for the drama as it is. Others believe that it is not the audience, not the creators, but rather the networks followed by the sponsors and the affiliates which control television. However, regardless of how control is perceived, the content is clearly the result of continuing struggles and conflicts, not simply demand (Cantor, 1979a, 1979b). Although television drama would no doubt be different if it were not for the capitalist system as it has evolved in the United States, it must be recognized that the drama has a long tradition in western society. It not only changes, but also remains the same. And as Todd Gitlin has noted, tastes are not entirely manufactured. That the audience accepts the system as it is exists and that drama continues to be profitable cannot be denied. Although the critics, some social scientists, pressure groups, and others define television drama as a public issue, the majority audience for drama remains silent, only turning the dial when programs are no longer appealing.

The question of whether the audience is being manipulated or harmed politically or psychologically cannot be answered by the kind of analysis presented here. There is no question that popular drama provides entertainment, possibly escape, and enjoyment for millions of people in the United States and abroad. Also, it is clear that, regardless of one's opinion that the audience is manipulated, helpless, or very powerful, the industrial structures define the audience and in turn the audience has the power to accept or reject the product.

NOTES

1. Most presentations of how feedback occurs are focused on the communicators (sources) and not necessarily on the receivers. Later in the chapter the concept of feedback will be discussed in more detail as it applies to television viewers.

2. A recent example of a movie which was previewed with two different endings before separate audiences is *Apocalypse Now.* In the heyday of Hollywood during the 1930s and 1940s, it was common practice to try out various endings before a film was released.

3. Fred Silverman, presently head of NBC television, has received much public attention for his success when he was in a similar position at ABC. He is considered to be responsible for ABC's position among the three networks. ABC for many years received the lowest ratings for its shows. After Silverman headed the network and was responsible for program selection, ABC became the top network.

7

SUMMARY AND POSSIBLE FUTURES

Speculation about the future of television drama within the
general framework of book. Suggestions for future research.

Throughout this book the dual nature of prime-time drama has been
emphasized. Television drama is both an art form and an economic
commodity. As both it is valued as a societal resource and thus has
generated an ongoing struggle for control and access among diverse
groups and coalitions. This struggle has taken place through the legal
system, through citizen group actions, and in the marketplace. To
explain how content is created and to document the struggle for its
control, the legal, social, and organizational context of production has
been examined.

Television drama is not simply a reflection of the tastes or values of
the creators (actors, directors, writers, and producers), nor is it simply
determined by economic factors. Rather, the content of television
drama represents a negotiated struggle and exchange among a number
of participants: the three major television networks, the Hollywood
program suppliers and their creative people, the United States government (especially the Federal Communications Commission and Congress), social critics, and citizen groups. The audience's role in this
struggle is problematic, as was explained in Chapter 6. Rather than the
audience initiating the drama, the viewing audience's power rests in its
ability to accept or reject what is presented.

As with all struggles, some participants have more power than
others. At the present time, the television networks are the most
powerful in determining the content of television drama. Supported by
the legal system, the networks have the power to decide what programs

will be presented to the audience, the time these programs will be broadcast, and whether the drama will be continued. However, the television networks do not exist in a social vacuum; they are dependent on program suppliers to provide the drama, local stations to broadcast programs, advertisers to sponsor their offerings, and rating services to evaluate their decisions. For local stations and advertisers to support the programs selected by the networks, a sufficiently large audience (determined by ratings) must tune in. Also, both advertisers and local stations may be intimidated by overt pressure from diverse citizen groups. Before a program is selected by the networks, two questions are usually asked: What will certain groups do if the program is aired. Will the audience like the show?

Television dramatic content, although the product of decisions by network officials and program suppliers, overall is consistent with public norms, evasive where there is overt controversy, and supportive of the economic interests of the industry where they are clear (Comstock et al., 1978:83). As to be expected, network officials and program suppliers are more comfortable with programs that have met with audience approval. Innovation and change are not rewarded; rather, trusted formulas, themes and formats are encouraged. Under the system that has developed (and is still developing) since 1954 when Hollywood became the major production for drama, most shows are standardized and considered low brow. Many analysts, when discussing television drama, view the content as unchanging, supporting the status quo, and often deleterious in its effects on the audience.

However, when the content of television drama is scrutinized, some changes in both form and message can be detected. The content of drama has clearly changed since the early days of television, but not in the direction desired by some critics. The exact nature of the changes are unclear and only certain types can be documented. The most important change is the replacement of action/adventure series with situation comedies as the most common form of television drama. This change is the direct result of the pressure from such groups as Action for Children's Television, the Parent-Teacher Association, and the American Medical Association who protested vigorously to have violent content removed (or reduced) from television. In place of the action programs which enjoyed very high ratings from the audience, new forms of dramatic television have been introduced: movies made for television and miniseries. These programs are often violent, but they are not on the air on a weekly basis and thus are less likely to be subjected to continued pressure from critics. The situation comedies and serialized evening shows now popular present a different picture of American life than do the action/adventure series. Sexual intimacy is more prevalent, family life less traditional, and more women and minority members are seen on the air. Some contend that these changes are cosmetic because the basic myths and power relationships presented are similar whether the shows are situation comedies or action series. The documentation for such claims is weak; few have examined the content systematically for basic ideology. There have been few analyses comparing themes, plots, and social relationships in television drama from its beginnings to the present. The one systematic analysis done by Lynda Glennon and Richard Butsch (1978) shows that working-class lifestyles were presented differently in drama during the 1950s when compared with similar programming in the 1970s.

Most critics of television drama (and there are many) are not interested in the changes noted from this analysis. The cultural content, although the subject of many controversies, is considered basically bad no matter how it changes. As discussed in detail in Chapter 2, most investigators of the content start from the position that television drama contains negative symbols, and therefore do not seriously consider questions of changing formula or whether changing values are being presented in the drama. Their major contribution to knowledge about the content has been to examine how series and other dramas present men and women, minorities, occupational roles, violence, and, more recently, sex.

Because of the popularity of television drama with the audience, it should be taken seriously as a form of culture. As Herbert Gans has pointed out, critics have been dismissing most popular art forms as low level and without artistic merit and therefore not worthy of serious consideration. The literature on popular culture, until very recently, has been written from an elitist position. The critics know what is "good" for the masses, and almost all arguments against television drama and other popular arts, as Horace Newcomb (1974) and Herbert Gans (1974) have both noted, have been arguments against the audience or against the system in which the arts are created. The mass society critics in particular believe that all popular culture has its own genuine characteristics: standardization, stereotypy, conservatism, mendacity, and manipulated consumer good (Rosenberg and White, 1957). All popular art forms are considered vulgar and unaesthetic. They function as means of keeping the masses narcotized, ineffectual in the political process, distracted, and entertained. Individual creativity is devalued. The system operates only for profit, and therefore the creators become workers on a mass assembly line who give up the expressions of their own skills and values.

The major result of the criticism is to ignore the content and to consider popular culture just a commodity that has negative effects on the audience. Other art forms also qualify as salable commodities: the motion picture, the pop music recording, fiction (especially romance, dime novels, and mysteries), comic books, and many others. All have been similarly criticized but not as extensively as has television drama. Two qualities distinguish television drama from other popular art forms: the size of the audience it can command and the nature of the criticism it generates. Although a book can be read or a movie seen by millions over time, a story transmitted through television is seen simultaneously by hundreds of millions of people. For example, 150 million Americans watched one or more episodes of *Roots* during the week of January 20, 1977; *Bonanza,* which was syndicated almost worldwide, claimed a weekly audience of that number during the 1968-1969 season. Although *Gone With the Wind* was one of the greatest box office successes compared with other films, it drew more people during the two nights it was shown on television for the first time than from all its movie showings combined. No phonograph record, novel, theater film, or any other form of popular art can compare with television in the size of the audience it can reach.

Other kinds of television programs also draw large audiences. It is the nature of the medium. However, 34 of the 53 top-rated shows in television reported by the A.C. Nielsen Company from July 1960 through January 1977 were series or miniseries episodes. Overall, drama accounted for 39 of the 53 programs. The other dramas on the list were movies made originally for theater distribution (Fireman, 1977:304).

The other quality that distinguishes television drama from other popular art forms is the amount of criticism it generates. As noted earlier, all popular culture has its critics. As each form of popular culture in turn becomes the mass medium for its generation, it also becomes the focus for criticism. Movies, radio, comic books, and other forms of popular fiction have each been criticized similarly to television drama.

The criticism generated by television has been quantitatively more extensive—it never seems to end (see Asashina, 1979 for a recent review). The criticism seems to be qualitatively different as well. The industry, the production companies, the advertisers, the content, and the medium itself are under constant barrage. However, in spite of all the criticism and research associated with the criticism, television drama remains low level and standardized. Although sociologists are not supposed to make aesthetic evaluations about art, by commonly accepted standards applied to the fine arts and to drama generally, most television fare does not qualify as fine art.

Many critics of television are social scientist who use empirical findings to justify their remarks. Although not everyone is convinced, many thoughtful investigators believe that television is a major agent of socialization (Comstock et al., 1978:285). George Gerbner claims that heavy viewing of television induces exaggerated senses of danger, mistrust, and vulnerability (Gerbner et al., 1977). In spite of the criticism, authoritative research, and pressure from such established groups as the Parent-Teacher Association and the American Medical Association, the content of television drama has not changed in the desired directions. Also, the popularity of television drama remains high with the audience. As suggested earlier, pressure groups have had some effect on the content and form of the drama being discussed, but essentially their power is limited by the nature of control and the organizational imperatives of work.

TECHNOLOGY AND CHANGE

Almost everything being written about television in recent years suggests that we are on the verge of a communications revolution involving the adoption of new technologies for the transmission of information and entertainment. Many of these technologies, such as cable and videotape recorders, have been available for many years, but due to legal encumbrances and business reluctance to invest in their manufacture, they have not been available nationwide. However, there is evidence that during the 1980s both cable and recording equipment will become generally more available. Some claim this availability will provide a greater choice of drama for the audience, more work for creative people, and new forms of dramatic production.

Although predicting the future is always risky, I will predict that dramatic offerings will indeed change. The production of most series and serial drama will remain under network control. There will be more choices for home viewing, but this will not be through network television. As cable becomes available in more cities, no doubt one or more channels will be for pay television. These channels will provide movies previously shown in the movie theaters and possible some new productions and videotapes of live theater. These options are presently available for several million viewers nationally. Because the law requires that minority groups have access to one of the many channels available through cable, there will also be more minority productions. In addition, there may be more drama presented on public television. Thus, more segments of the audience will be able to choose between network offerings and other kinds of television drama.

Although these alternative sources of programming will be available, the networks will continue to transmit and finance many dramatic productions. The target audience for network drama is the lower middle class, those between the ages of 18 and 49 who are married with children. This group represents the largest segment of the population for the 1980s. Many people in that group are unlikely to subscribe to pay television in large numbers when they can get appealing programs without paying. The networks with sponsor support will be able to continue to generate profits even if the audience shrinks slightly or remains stable. For example, the soap opera audience appears to have stabilized or possibly contracted in recent years as more women in the target audience enter the labor force. However, daytime television continues to be very profitable for the networks (Cantor 1979a). Even if half the homes in the country have pay television available and others (or the same people) have home video tape or video disc as well, the networks will be able to attract enough people to make dramatic television profitable.

How will competition from other means of dissemination change television drama content? I do not know. It is likely that instead of less sensationalism, violence, and sex there will be more. Producers and network officials believe that sex and violence sells. Also, network television drama will not be obligated to present even token drama that is considered high quality since that drama will be available from other sources. It is likely that increasing competition among the networks for a constant or shrinking audience will also enhance the power of the rating services.

The greatest changes from the adoption of new means of dissemination will be in the production companies. These changes will mean more and varied kinds of production. However, the changes probably will not help the movie industry in Hollywood itself because most drama can be made on location, either in the United States or abroad. If there is more work for actors and writers, this work might be available outside Los Angeles. However, the power of actors (other than stars) and writers will not increase. The established and supported production companies and some producers may gain independence, but the chances for entry into production for newcomers will remain slim, as always. Production will continue to be concentrated in the hands of a few program suppliers who will be able to put more programs into production. The situation will remain the same for writers, directors, and actors. Although program suppliers may have more control, when they are dependent on others to finance and distribute their products, they almost always lose some creative freedom.

There is disagreement about the future uses of the television screens. Others do not agree that alternatives to network television will mean more diversity and pluralism in programming. However, there is general agreement among financial experts that these alternatives will not spell doom for the three television network (Weintraub, 1979). Most Americans probably will continue to choose network television as the medium of their choice for both entertainment and information. Because the number of households will grow substantially in the next few years, the number of viewers of commercial television are likely to remain constant, although some viewers will be diverted elsewhere. Because the networks will continue to attract most of the advertising dollars with their large national audiences, their power over producers will remain substantial. The profit associated with successful television drama will continue to attract program suppliers, who will try to have their products disseminated through the networks.

The present system favors the networks rather than the production companies. Another reason for network power is that the networks can afford some failures which the production companies cannot. According to *Newsweek* (1979), almost no other industry can match prime-time television's record of failure. Up to this point in the discussion, much emphasis has been given to the success associated with certain shows. However, television is a high-risk business. Not a single one of the 22 series that went on the air in September 1979 made the Nielsen top ten list by December (*Newsweek*, 1979). Instead, most were at the bottom and many were dropped by January 1980. The networks are not particularly skilled at gauging what will appeal to the large target audience. However, to maintain profits, they need not have a high success rate. Shows are simply dropped and replaced on the schedule with new offerings. Individual network officials may be demoted or fired if too many shows fail, but the networks continue to secure support from advertisers and thus maintain high profits. Of course, a high success rate is better than a low one. Networks prefer successful programs because they bring more revenues and keep affiliates happy.

Those who suffer most from the high failure rate are the program suppliers and the creative people working on unsuccessful series. When a show is cancelled the production companies usually have to stop production and lose the chance of the program becoming syndicated. Although production people protest the network's control, claiming their artistic freedom is being jeopardized, at the present time to be successful, a production company must have support from the network. Some claim the new diversity will bring this desired freedom, but most realize their major support will continue to come from the networks. Rather than changing television from a mass medium, most simply desire artistic control, claiming they, not the networks, can better judge what will appeal to the audience.

CONCLUSION

The content of drama, both form and actual message, seems to depend on social and political conditions existing outside the creative process. The power of the networks remains the primary control on the creators, but critics and social action groups, through continuing pressure, have increased the government's involvement in television production.

If one believes that creative people should have freedom and autonomy, the prospects for more creative control at the inception of production remain dismal. It is clear from the history of broadcasting and film that regulation is not static; changes come both from congressional action and from court decisions. There has been little governmental participation in creation, but its role in this area has been increasing. It is doubtful, however, that the law will contribute to more diversity in programming from the networks. The changes in the law concerning cable and pay television in the last ten years will contribute to more diversity. However, diversity may be only the choice of the well-to-do and the educated. Regardless of what kinds of films are to be produced in the future, those who will control the means of dissemination, rather than the writers, actors, and directors, will have the power to decide what is to be produced.

POSTSCRIPT

People who like television drama can expect to see more of the same in the near future. It seems that all audiences have to do is keep their sets on. However, if one would like to contribute some input into the creative process, the choice of action is problematic. Becoming part of an action group could be the answer. Critics have been instrumental in effecting some changes, but the changes have been limited. Also there is some evidence that pressure groups have become tired, and their power is more limited now than it has been in the recent past.

If one is a network official, the problem is to figure out how to choose successful programs. It appears that market research is little help in the selection process. If one is a program supplier, clearly both the networks and the new markets must be approached with fresh ideas and concepts. If one is an actor, writer, or director, seeking work, increasing skills, and good luck may bring desired success. For most failure is inevitable. There is no way demand for workers can increase to meet the supply of creative people available. Some believe that the truly creative and talented are eventually able to find fame and fortune through drama. However, for every actor who is able to work in films, at least 100 have failed. The talents of many under such a system must go unrecognized.

If one is a researcher, many questions remain unanswered. As popular as prime-time drama is, the knowledge about the content is fragmentary. As far as I know, almost no comparative studies have been conducted on the content of movies, plays, and television drama. More content analyses should be forthcoming as well as more systematic literary analyses. For example, the history of western drama, including television in perspective, should be undertaken. Moreover, the content should never be studied outside the social context in which it is created. An industry-wide study which examines not only the business aspects of broadcasting and filmmaking but also the craft aspects is necessary.

This study would relate the expansion and contraction of creative work to business practices, to the selection process of content, and to power relationships in the industry. The dual nature of popular drama must be reconciled. It is likely that all highly profitable popular art forms generate a struggle and exchange between the creators and those outside the actual creative process.

BIBLIOGRAPHY

Ad Hoc Committee on Alcohol and the Media (1976) Meeting transcript. Washington, DC: National Institute on Alcohol Abuse and Alcoholism. (mimeo)

American Business Consultants (1950) "Red channels." Counterattack: The Newsletter of Facts to Combat Communism. New York: American Business Consultants.

ANDREWS, B. W. (1978) Fiction in the United States: An Ideological Medium Supporting Capitalism? M. A. thesis, Department of Sociology, American University, Washington, D. C. (unpublished)

ASASHINA, R. (1979) "Blame it on the tube." Harpers (November): 106-111.

AVERY, I. (1977) "The golden age of TV drama," pp. 71-74 in J. Fireman (ed.) TV Book: The Ultimate Television Book. New York: Workman.

BARAN, S. J. (1976a) "Sex on TV and adolescent sexual self-image." Journal of Broadcasting 20, 1: 57-81.

——— (1976b) 'How TV and film portrayals affect sexual satisfaction in college students." Journalism Quarterly 53, 3: 468-473.

BARNOUW, E. (1978) The Sponsor: Notes on a Modern Potentate. New York: Oxford University Press.

——— (1977) Tube of Plenty: The Evolution of American Television. New York: Oxford University Press

——— (1970) The Image Empire: A History of Broadcasting in the United States from 1953. New York: Oxford University Press.

BAUER, R. (1958) "The communicator and the audience." Conflict Resolution 2: 66-78.

BELL, D. (1961) The End of Ideology. New York: Collier Books.

BOGART L. (1972) "Warning, the Surgeon General has determined that TV violence is moderately dangerous to your child's mental health." Public Opinion Quarterly 36, 4: 491-521.

BRAMSON, L. (1961) The Political Context of Sociology. Princeton: Princeton University Press.

BREED, W. (1955) "Social control in the newsroom: a functional analysis." Social Forces 33: 326-335.

Brief for Appellants (1977) Writers Guild of America, Inc. et. al, Plaintiffs-Appellees, v. American Broadcasting Companies, Inc. et al, Defendants-Appellants. U. S. Court of Appeals, Ninth District, June 27.

Broadcasting (1974) "Producers gripped in new crunch between costs and prices." September 23: 15-17.

BROWN, L. (1971) Televi$ion: The Business Behind the Box. New York: Harcourt Brace Jovanovich.

CANTOR, M. G. (1979a) "Our days and our nights on TV." Journal of Communication 29 (Autumn): 66-72.

——— (1979b) "The politics of popular drama." Communication Research 6 (October): 387-406.

——— (1974) "Producing television for children," pp. 103-118 in G. Tuchman (ed.) The TV Establishment: Programming for Power and Profit. Englewood Cliffs, NJ. Prentice-Hall.

——— (1972) "The role of the producer in choosing children's television content," pp. 259-289 in G. A. Comstock and E. A. Rubinstein (eds.) Television and Social Behavior, Vol. I. Content and Control. Washington, DC: U.S. Government Printing Office.

——— (1971) The Hollywood TV Producer: His Work and His Audience. New York: Basic Books.

——— and A. K. PETERS (1979) "The employment and unemployment of screen actors in the United States." Presented at the First International Conference on Economics and the Arts, Edinburgh, Scotland, August 11. (Proceedings to be published by Abt Associates, Cambridge, MA)

CATER, D. and S. STRICKLAND (1975) TV Violence and The Child: The Evolution and Fate of The Surgeon General's Report. New York: Russell Sage.

CLARKE, P. (1978) "The sociology of literature: an historical introduction," pp. 237-258 in R. A. Jones (ed.) Research in Sociology of Knowledge, Sciences and Art, Vol. I. Greenwich, CT: JAI Press.

COMSTOCK, G., S. CHAFFEE, N. KATZMAN, M. McCOMBS, and D. ROBERTS (1978) Television and Human Behavior. New York: Columbia University Press.

DAVID, N. (1978) TV Season, 1976, 1977. Phoenix, AZ: Oryx Press.

——— (1977) TV Season, 1975, 1976. Phoenix, AZ: Oryx Press.

——— (1976) TV Season, 1974, 1975. Phoenix, Arizona: Oryx Press.

DeFLEUR, M. L. (1970) Theories of Mass Communication. New York: David McKay.

——— (1964) "Occupational roles as portrayed on television." Public Opinion Quarterly 28: 57-74.

——— and S. BALL-ROKEACH (1975) Theories of Mass Communication. New York: David McKay.

del SOLA POOL, I. and I. SHULMAN (1964) "Newsmen's fantasies, audiences, and newswriting," pp. 141 159 in L. A. Dexter and D. M. White (eds.) People, Society, and Mass Communications. New York: Free Press.

DiMAGGIO, P. (1977) "Market structure, the creative process, and popular culture: toward an organizational reinterpretation of mass culture theory." Journal of Popular Culture 11: 436-467.

DOMMINICK, J. R. and M. C. PEARCE (1976) "Trends in network prime-time programming, 1953-74." Journal of Communication 26 (Winter): 70-80.

DUNNING, J. (1976) Tune In Yesterday: The Ultimate Encyclopedia of Old-Time Radio, 1925 1976. Englewood Cliffs, NJ: Prentice-Hall.

EISENHOWER, M. S. (1969) Commission Statement on Violence in Television

Entertainment Programs. Washington, DC: National Commission on the Causes and Prevention of Violence.

ELLIOT, P. (1972) The Making of a Television Series: A Case Study in the Sociology of Culture. New York: Hastings House.

ELLUL, J. (1964) The Technological Society. New York: Vintage Books.

FAULKNER, R. R. (1971) Hollywood Studio Musicians: Their Work and Careers in the Recording Industry. Chicago: AVC.

Federal Communications Commission (1971) The Communications Act of 1934 with Amendments and Indexes Thereto. Recapped to January 1969. Washington, DC: U.S. Government Printing Office.

Federal Register (1974) Fairness Doctrine and Public Interest Standards, pp. 26372-26390, 39,139 (July 18). Washington, DC: U.S. Government Printing Office.

FERNANDEZ-COLLADO, C. F. and B. S. GREENBERG (1978) "Sexual intimacy and drug use." Journal of Communication 28 (Summer): 30-37.

——— (1977) Substance Use and Sexual Intimacy on Commercial Television. East Lansing: Department of Communication, Michigan State University.

FIREMAN, J. [ed.] (1977) TV Book: The Ultimate Television Book. New York: Workman.

FRANZBLAU, S., J. N. SPRAFKIN, and E. A. RUBINSTEIN (1977) "Sex on TV: a content analysis " Journal of Communication 27 (Spring): 164-171.

FRANZWA, H. (1978) "The image of women in television: an annotated bibliography," pp. 272-300 in G. Tuchman, A. K. Daniels, and J. Benet (eds.) Hearth and Home: Images of Women in the Mass Media. New York: Oxford University Press.

FRIENDLY, F. W. (1975) The Good Guys, The Bad Guys and the First Amendment: Free Speech vs Fairness in Broadcasting. New York: Random House.

——— (1967) Due to Circumstances beyond Our Control. New York: Random House.

GANS, H. J. (1974) Popular Culture and High Culture. New York: Basic Books.

——— (1957) "The creator-audience relationship in the mass media: an analysis of movie making," pp. 315-324 in B. Rosenberg and D. White (eds.) Mass Culture: The Popular Arts in America. New York: Free Press.

GERBNER, G. (1972) "Violence in television drama: trends and symbolic functions," pp. 128-187 in G. S. Comstock and E. A. Rubinstein (eds.) Television and Social Behavior, Vol. I. Media Content and Control. Washington DC: U.S. Government Printing Office.

——— and L. GROSS (1979) "Editorial response: a reply to Newcomb's 'Humanistic Critique.' " Communication Research 6 (April): 223-230.

——— and N. SIGNORIELLI (1979) Aging with Television: Images of Television Drama and Conceptions of Social Reality: A Preview of the Final Report of a Research Conducted under a Grant from the Administration of Aging, Office of Human Development, Department of Health, Education and Welfare, Philadelphia: Annenberg School of Communication, University of Pennsylvania.

GERBNER, G., L. GROSS, M. F. ELEEY, M. JACKSON-BEECK, S. JEFFRIES-FOX, and N. SIGNORIELLI (1977) "TV violence profile no. 8: the highlights." Journal of Communication 27 (Spring): 171-180

GERBNER, G., L. GROSS, M. JACKSON-BEECK, S. JEFFRIES-FOX, and N. SIGNORIELLI (1978) Cultural indicators: violence profile no. 9. Journal of Communication 28(Summer): 176-207.

GITLIN, T. (1979) "Prime-time ideology: the hegemonic process in television entertainment." Social Problems 26(February): 251-266.

GLENNON, L. and R. BUTSCH (1978) "The devaluation of working class lifestyle in television family series, 1947-1977." (unpublished)

GOLDSEN, R. K. (1977) The Show and Tell Machine: How Television Works and Works You Over. New York: Dial Press.

GRAMSCIE, A. (1971) Selections from the Prison Notebooks (ed. and trans. by Q. Hoare and G. N. Smith; written between 1929 and 1935). New York: International Publishers.

HALL, S. (1974) "Media power: the double bind." Journal of Communication 24 (Autumn): 19-26.

HANKS, W. E. and T. A. PICKETT (1979) "Influence of community-based citizen groups on television broadcasters in five Eastern cities: an exploratory study," pp. 105-134 in H. S. Dordick (ed.) Proceedings of the Sixth Annual Telecommunications Policy Research Conference. Lexington, MA: D. C. Heath.

HEAD, S. W. (1976) Broadcasting in America. Boston: Houghton-Mifflin.

——— (1954) "Content of television dramatic programs." Quarterly of Films, Radio and Television 9: 175 194.

HIRSCH, P. M. (1978a) "Occupational, organizational and institutional models in mass media research," pp. 13-42 in P. Hirsch, P. Miller, and F. G. Kline (eds.) Strategies for Mass Communication Research. Beverly Hills, CA: Sage.

——— (1978b) "Production and distribution of roles among cultural organizations: on the division of labor across intellectual disciplines." Social Research 45: 316-328. (special issue on book publishing)

——— (1972) "Processing fads and fashions: an organizational set analysis of culture industry systems." American Journal of Sociology 77 (January): 639-659.

HORKHEIMER, M. and T. W. ADORNO (1972) Dialectic of Enlightenment. New York: Herder and Herder.

HOWARD, N. (1979) "The TV networks under pressure." Dunn's Review (January).

JANUS, N. (1977) "Research on sex-roles in the mass media: toward a critical approach." The Insurgent Sociologist 7 (Summer): 19-32.

JOHNSTONE, J.W.C., E. J. SLAWSKI, and W. W. BOWMAN (1976) The News People: A Sociological Portrait of American Journalists and Their Work. Urbana: University of Illinois Press.

KATZ, E. (1977) Social Research on Broadcasting: Proposals for Further Development. Produced by the Publicity and Information Department. British Broadcasting Corporation.

KORNHAUSER, W. (1959) The Politics of Mass Society. New York: Free Press.

KRASNOW, E. G. and L. D. Longley (1973) The Politics of Broadcast Regulation. New York: St. Martin's.

LASSWELL, H. D. (1966) "Nations and classes: the symbols of identification," pp. 27-42 in B. Berelson and M. Janowitz (eds.) Reader in Public Opinion and Communication. New York: Free Press.

LEIFER, A. D., N. J. GORDON, and S. B. GRAVES (1974) "Children's television: more than mere entertainment." Harvard Educational Review 44: 213-245.

LEMON, J. (1978) "Dominant or dominated? women on prime-time television," pp. 51-68 in G. Tuchman, A. K. Daniels, and J. Benet (eds.) Hearth and Home: Images of Women in the Mass Media. New York: Oxford University Press.

LEWIS, G. H. (1978) The Sociology of Popular Culture. Current Sociology 26 (Winter).

LIEBERT, R., J. M. NEALE, and E. S. DAVIDSON (1973) The Early Window: Effects of Television on Children and Youth. New York: Pergammon Press.

LIPPMANN, W. (1959) "The problem of television." New York Herald Tribune, October 27.

LYLE, J. (1974) The People Look at Public Television. Washington, DC: Corporation for Public Broadcasting.

McQUAIL, D. (1969) Towards a Sociology of Mass Communications. London: Collier-Macmillan.

MANDER, J. (1978) Four Arguments for the Elimination of Television. New York: Morrow Quill.

MANKIEWICZ, F. and J. SWERDLOW (1978) Remote Control: Television and the Manipulation of American Life. New York: Times Books.

MARCUSE, H. (1964) One-Dimensional Man: Studies in the Ideology of Advanced Industrial Society. Boston: Beacon.

MARX, K. and F. ENGELS (1962) Selected Works, Vol. 1. Moscow: Foreign Languages Publishing House.

MAYER, M. (1979) "Summing up the seventies—television." American Film 3 (December): 27, 53-55.

MELODY, W. (1973) Children's Television: The Economics of Exploitation. New Haven, CT: Yale University Press.

MIELKE, K. W., R. C. JOHNSON, and B. G. COLE (1975) Federal Role in Funding Children's Television Programming. Bloomington: Institute for Communication Research, Department of Telecommunications, Indiana University.

MILLER, M. and E. RHODES (1964) Only You, Dick Daring! New York: William Sloane.

MILLS, C. W. (1953) White Collar. New York: Oxford University Press.

MINNOW, N. (1973) "Preface," in E. G. Krasnow and L. D. Longley (eds.) The Politics of Broadcast Regulation. New York: St. Martin's.

MOORE, J. (1961) "Occupational anomie and irresponsibility." Social Problems 8, 2: 293-299.

——— (n.d.) "The Hollywood writer." (unpublished manuscript)

NEA (1976) Employment and Unemployment of Artists, 1970-75. Washington, DC: National Endowment for the Arts.

NEWCOMB, H. (1978) "Assessing the violence profile studies of Gerbner and Gross: a humanistic critique and suggestion." Communication Research 5(July): 264-282.

——— (1974) TV: The Most Popular Art. New York: Doubleday. *Newsweek*

Newsweek (1979) "Producers in revolt." December 10: 126-129.

NOW (1972) Women in the Wasteland Fight Back. Washington: National Organization for Women.

PETERS, A. K. and M. G. CANTOR (1978) "Acting as work." Presented at the annual meeting of the Southern Sociological Society, New Orleans, Louisiana, April 1. (unpublished)

PETERSON, R. A. (1976) "The production of Culture: a prolegomenon." American Behavioral Scientist 19: 669-685.

PHILLIPS K. (1977) "Busting the media trusts." Harpers (July): 23-34.

Red Lion Broadcasting, Inc. v. FCC (1969) Supreme Court of the United States 395 US 367, April 2.

Report of the United States Commission on Civil Rights (1979) Window Dressing on the Set: An Update. Washington, DC: U.S. Government Printing Office.

——— (1977) Window Dressing on the Set. Washington, DC: U.S. Government Printing Office.

RILEY, J. and M. RILEY (1959) "Mass communication and the social system," pp. 537-578 in R. K. Merton, L. Broom, and L. S. Cottrell, Jr. (eds.) Sociology Today. New York: Basic Books.

ROBINSON, M. J. (1979) "Prime-time chic: between newsbreaks and commercials. the values are L. A. liberal." Public Opinion 2 (March/May): 42-47.

ROSENBERG, B. (1957) "Mass culture in America," pp. 3-11 in B. Rosenberg and D. M. White (eds.) Mass Culture: The Popular Arts in America. New York: Free Press.

——— and D. M. WHITE (1957) Mass Culture: The Popular Arts in America. New York: Free Press.

SALLACH, D. L. (1974) "Class domination and ideological hegemony," pp. 161-173 in G. Tuchman (ed.) The TV Establishment. Englewood Cliffs, NJ: Prentice-Hall.

SANDMAN, P. M., D. M. RUBIN, and D. B. SACHSMAN (1972) Media. Englewood Cliffs NJ: Prentice-Hall.

SCHILLER, H. I. (1969) Mass Communications and American Empire. New York: Augustus M. Kelley.

SCHRAMM, W. (1973) Men, Messages and Media: A Look at Human Communications. New York: Harper & Row.

SCHUMACH, M. (1964) The Face on the Cutting Room Floor: The Story of Movie and Television Censorship. New York: William Morrow.

SEGGAR, J. and P. WHEELER (1973) "World of work on TV: ethnic and sex representations in TV drama." Journal of Broadcasting 17: 201-214.

SEIDEN, M. H. (1974) "Who Controls the Mass Media? Popular Myths and Economic Realities. New York: Basic Books.

SELDES, G. (1964) The Public Arts. New York: Simon and Schuster.

SILVERMAN, L. T., J. N. SPRAFKIN, and E. A. RUBINSTEIN (1979) "Physical contact and sexual behavior on prime-time TV." Journal of Communication 29 (Winter): 33-43.

SKORNIA, J (1967) Public Television: A Program for Action. New York: Bantam Books.

SPILBECK, O. (1960) ABC of Film and TV Working Terms. New York: Focal Press.

STEDMAN, R. W. (1977) The Serials: Suspense and Drama by Installments. Norman: Oklahoma Press.

STEIN, B. (1979) The View from Sunset Strip: America as Brought by the People Who Make Television. New York: Basic Books.

STEINBERG, C. S. (1970) The Communicative Arts: An Introduction to Mass Media. New York: Hasting House.

STERLING, C. K. and T. R. HAIGHT (1978) The Mass Media: Aspen Institute Guide to Communication Industry Trends. New York: Praeger.

STEWART, P. L. and M. G. CANTOR (1974) Varieties of Work Experiences. Cambridge, MA: Schenkman.

STINCHOMBE, A. L. (1959) "Bureaucratic and craft administration of production: a comparative study." Administrative Science Quarterly 4: 168-187.

Surgeon General's Scientific Advisory Committee on Television and Social Behavior (1972) Television and Growing Up: The Impact of Televised Violence: Report to the Surgeon General, United States Public Health Service. Washington, DC: U.S. Government Printing Office.

SWINGEWOOD, A. (1977) The Myth of Mass Culture. London: Macmillan.

TERRACE, V. (1976a) The Complete Encyclopedia of Television Programs, 1947-1976. Volume 1 A-K. New York: A. S. Barnes.

——— (1976b) The Complete Encyclopedia of Television Programs, 1947-1976. Volume II L-Z. New York: A. S. Barnes.

TUCHMAN, G. (1978) Making News: A Study in the Contruction of Reality. New York: Free Press.

——— (1974) "Introduction," pp. 1-40 in G. Tuchman (ed.) The TV Establishment. Englewood, Cliffs, NJ: Prentice-Hall

TUNSTALL, J. (1977) The Media are American: Anglo-American Media are American. New York: Columbia University Press.

TUROW J. (1978) 'Personal correspondence." January 28.

TV Guide (1977) "Sex and violence: Hollywood fights back." August 27: 4-18.

U.S. Congress, House (1979) Communications Act of 1979. H.R. 3333, 96th Congress, First Session.

——— (1977) Violence on Television. Report by the Subcommittee on Communications of the Committee on Interstate and Foreign Commerce. 95th Congress, First Session. September 29.

U.S. Congress, Senate (1979) A Bill to Amend the Communications Act of 1934. S 249 96th Congress, First Session.

Wall Street Journal (1979) "Plan to overhaul communications law is being abandoned by House panels " July 16.

WELLS, A. (1972) Picture-Tube Imperialism? The Impact of U.S. Television on Latin-America. Maryknoll, NY: Orbis Books.

WEINTRAUB, B. (1979) "The whole idea of TV may change." Washington *Star*, December 12: C-2.

WILLIAMS, R. (1977) Marxism and Literature. Oxford, England: Oxford University Press.

WINICK, C. (1959) Taste and the Censor in Television. New York: Fund for the
    Republic, Inc.
WINN, M. (1977) The Plug In Drug. New York: Viking.
WRIGHT, C. R. (1975) Mass Communications: A Sociological Perspective. New
    York: Random House.
Writers Guild of America, West v. FCC (1976) No. CV 75-3641-F.

INDEX

ABOUT THE AUTHOR

MURIEL G. CANTOR has a Ph.D. in sociology from the University of California, Los Angeles. As part of her doctoral work, she wrote her dissertation on the sociology of television producers. Since that time (1969) she has been investigating various aspects of primetime drama, how it is created, by whom, and under what conditions. Her published works on the subject have appeared in *Communication Research, Journal of Communication, Journalism Quarterly,* and in several collections of readings. Her book *The Hollywood TV Producer* and the book she co-edited with Phyllis Stewart, *Varieties of Work Experience,* provide the analytical framework for the present volume. She has been a consultant for the Corporation for Public Broadcasting, the National Institute of Mental Health, the Office of Education, and the National Organization for Women on the subjects of sex-role portrayals and employment of women in broadcasting. In addition, she was a contributor to the Report to the Surgeon General on Television and Social Behavior. She is presently Professor of Sociology at American University, Washington, D.C., where she was former Chair of the Department. As principal investigator for a grant from the National Institute of Mental Health on "Sex and Sexual Violence in Women's Fiction," she will be watching less television and reading more fiction.